HOW TO BECOME
FAMOUS

HOW TO BECOME
FAMOUS

Lost Einsteins, Forgotten Superstars, and How the Beatles Came to Be

CASS R. SUNSTEIN

HARVARD BUSINESS REVIEW PRESS

BOSTON, MASSACHUSETTS

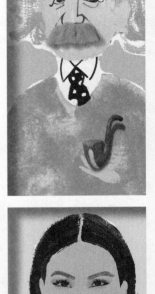

Library of Congress Cataloging-in-Publication Data

Names: Sunstein, Cass R., author.
Title: How to become famous: lost Einsteins, forgotten superstars, and how the Beatles came to be / Cass R. Sunstein.
Description: Boston, Massachusetts : Harvard Business Review Press, [2023] | Includes index. |
Identifiers: LCCN 2023046080 (print) | LCCN 2023046081 (ebook) | ISBN 9781647825362 (hardcover) | ISBN 9781647825379 (epub)
Subjects: LCSH: Success. | Fame.
Classification: LCC BJ1611.2 .S825 2023 (print) | LCC BJ1611.2 (ebook) | DDC 650.1092/2--dc23/eng/20231220
LC record available at https://lccn.loc.gov/2023046080
LC ebook record available at https://lccn.loc.gov/2023046081

ISBN: 978-1-64782-536-2
eISBN: 978-1-64782-537-9

To Samantha Power

So you want to be a rock 'n' roll star?
Then listen now to what I say
Just get an electric guitar
Then take some time and learn how to play

—The Byrds

The race is not to the swift, nor the battle to the strong, neither bread to the wise, nor yet riches to men of understanding, nor yet favor to men of skill; but time and chance happeneth to them all.

—Ecclesiastes

Interviewer: I find that you really have no idea as to why you are popular, no thoughts on why you are popular.

Bob Dylan: I just haven't really struggled for that. It happened, you know? It happened like anything else happens. Just a happening. You don't try to figure out happenings. You dig happenings. So I'm not going to even talk about it.

CONTENTS

The Crossroads

I t is February 9, 1964.

About 73 million Americans are huddled around their television sets. They are on edge. They are full of anticipation. They are watching the first live performance on American soil of a new musical group. The group has an unlikely name: the Beatles.

At the age of 23, John Lennon and Ringo Starr are the oldest. Paul McCartney is 21. George Harrison is just 20. The young musicians are appearing on the Ed Sullivan Show, a popular but stodgy entertainment series. In the studio itself, 728 tickets were sold; there had been 50,000 requests.[1]

Ed Sullivan introduces the performers:

Now yesterday and today our theater's been jammed with newspapermen and hundreds of photographers from all over the nation, and these veterans agreed with me that this city never has witnessed the excitement stirred by these youngsters from Liverpool who call themselves the Beatles. Now tonight, you're gonna twice be entertained by them. Right now, and again in the second half of our show. Ladies and gentlemen, the Beatles! Let's bring them on.[2]

Prologue

The group begins with "All My Loving," sung by McCartney: "Close your eyes and I'll kiss you/Tomorrow I'll miss you." The teenage girls in the audience shriek and scream. They scream so loud that McCartney is nearly drowned out. Members of the group smile and look up at the frenzied crowd in amazement, even disbelief.

The disbelief is understandable. Just a little more than two years before, the Beatles had repeatedly failed to get a record deal in England. No one would sign them. They were not so far from giving up.

Some people are struck by lightning. The Beatles were struck by lightning, and so was Taylor Swift, and so was Bob Dylan. So was Leonardo da Vinci, and so was Jane Austen, and so was William Blake. So was Steve Jobs, and so was Johann Sebastian Bach, and so was Barack Obama.

Some people are not struck by lightning, which is why you have not heard of them. As Benjamin Franklin put it, "There have been as great souls unknown to fame as any of the most famous."[3]

There are lost Beatles, lost Swifts, lost Dylans, lost da Vincis, lost Austens, lost Blakes, lost Jobses, lost Bachs, and lost Obamas— people of extraordinary talent who never got a chance, and hence were never struck by lightning, or people who were once struck by lightning, and hence got a chance, but who have been forgotten and lost. Some people are struck by lightning after their death. (Bach is an example, and so is Margaret Cavendish, on whom more later.)

Of course the idea of being struck by lightning is a mere metaphor, and it must be taken to include a whole host of twists and turns: where you were born, when you were born, whom you happened to encounter, who happened to encourage you, who enraged you, who helped you, who inspired you, who smiled at you, with whom you fell in love, with whom you didn't fall in love, who gave you a link or a megaphone (or a contract), whether you benefited from some kind of bandwagon effect, and who happened to promote you.

One twist is not like another twist. One turn is not like another turn. And for every encounter and inspiration and smile, there is a non-encounter, an inspiration that didn't happen, a blank stare, a distracted look, a link that wasn't, or a grimace.

One of my aims here is to emphasize the crucial role of serendipity and luck, which means that it is a mistake to attribute spectacular success to the intrinsic qualities of those who succeed. Of course, it is true that those who succeed might well be extraordinary. The Beatles were extraordinary, and so is Taylor Swift. Of course, it is true that without their extraordinariness, they might not have gotten very far.

But how did they become extraordinary? In what way did they get extraordinary? In any case, their extraordinariness was hardly sufficient to get them where they ended up. Countless extraordinary people, in business, politics, science, and the arts, never get very far. I also aim to open up the black box of serendipity and see what we might find there. To some extent, at least, serendipity can be engineered.

Here is one way to think about it. Life is a series of lotteries. All of us have entered a large number of them without knowing it. You are in a bunch of lotteries at this very moment. What ticket will you draw? With respect to fame, some people draw winning tickets. A lot of that is simple luck. Still, it is possible to increase one's chances.

The topic of fame is intriguing in itself, not least because of its overlap with the even larger topic of "success." I will have something to say about both. It is tempting to focus on what's hot, or on some vehicle or trend of the last year, month, week, or day: the latest social media platform, some new technology, some new scandal, the sudden emergence of a new face, some exceptional talent, something bright and shiny, some talentless wonder. But humanity has not changed, not really, and the general principles and mechanisms that I will discuss here are as old as our species and as new as the day after tomorrow.

As we shall see, the topic of fame is also a window onto a host of the most fundamental issues, involving memory, business, culture, sports, politics, science, and (emphatically) religion. The rise of Christianity will make an appearance here, and so will Gnosticism, Genghis Khan, the Holocaust, Virginia Woolf, Albert Einstein, Barbie, Martin Luther King Jr., Muhammad Ali, Stephen King, Oprah Winfrey, and Spider-Man.

Bob Dylan refused to say why he had become popular: "You don't try to figure out happenings. You dig happenings. So I'm not going to even talk about it." With respect, Mr. Dylan: You try to figure out happenings. So I'm going to talk about it.

Infatuation

In the middle of the eighteenth century, Samuel Johnson, author of the first English-language dictionary and *The Lives of the Poets*, had a great deal to say about lightning, fame, and infatuation. He emphasized that people are busy and that it is hard to get their attention. For that reason, "no man can be formidable, but to a small part of his fellow-creatures."[4]

Even worse, almost everyone is rapidly forgotten, even if they become famous during their lifetime. Speaking of writers in particular, Johnson said, "If we look back into past times, we find innumerable names of authors once high in reputation, read perhaps by the beautiful, quoted by the witty, and commented by the grave, but of whom we now know only that they once existed."[5] Johnson was right, but he understated it. We might not even know that they existed.

Johnson drew a sharp distinction between fame in one's lifetime and lasting fame. With respect to short-term renown, Johnson counseled skepticism. Johnson pointed to the "bubbles of artificial fame, which are kept up a while by a breath of fashion, and then break at once and are annihilated."[6] If we could retrieve the works of ancient writers, famous in their time and now lost, Johnson thought that we would be unimpressed. We would ask: Why did anyone think they were special? How on earth did they ever get famous? In Johnson's account, we would "wonder by what infatuation or caprice they could be raised to notice."[7]

Infatuation and caprice define fame during one's lifetime. The verdict of the long term is, in Johnson's view, far more reliable.

Johnson's favorite example? William Shakespeare. One reason is that he was an incomparable genius. Another is that his work speaks of enduring things, relevant not only to his time and place but more broadly to our species. At the same time, Johnson recognized that even enduring fame is a complicated thing. Speaking of Shakespeare, Johnson wrote, "Yet it must be at last confessed, that as we owe everything to him, he owes something to us; that, if much of his praise is paid by perception and judgment, much is likewise given by custom and veneration."[8] Johnson continued: "We fix our eyes upon his graces, and turn them from his deformities, and endure in him what we should in another loathe and despise."[9] That's a bit like being in love, isn't it?

Johnson used the term "bubbles," and so do we. We use it to refer to artificially inflated prices or popularity, often produced by a sense, on the part of numerous people, that *other* people like the product or person in question. It is easy to find real estate bubbles; pop singer bubbles; podcast bubbles; laptop bubbles; television show bubbles; stock bubbles, even stock market bubbles; movie star bubbles; novelist bubbles; and online magazine bubbles.

Bubbles pop. Yesterday's icon is tomorrow's flop. (That's the theme of Bob Dylan's "Like a Rolling Stone": "Ah you never turned around to see the frowns/On the jugglers and the clowns when they all did tricks for you.") In Johnson's view, fame is often a kind of bubble, and it is a product of infatuation or caprice.

Johnson thought that we should trust the long term. Should we?

Citizen Kane is often said to be the greatest movie ever made. In 1942, it lost the Oscar to *How Green Was My Valley*.[10] Does anyone remember *How Green Was My Valley*?

The Dave Clark Five were an immensely popular group in the early 1960s, often compared to their great rival, the Beatles. Music magazines devoted many pages to the intensely disputed question of which group was better. In 1964, an entire magazine was published with the name, *Dave Clark 5 vs. the Beatles*. The cover quoted Ringo as saying, "They're just imitations!"—and Dave Clark saying, "I'll duel with Ringo!" The Dave Clark Five have sold more than 100 million records.

I remember the Dave Clark Five well; they are scandalously underrated. "Glad All Over" is terrific, and "Bits and Pieces" and "I Like It Like That" are irresistible, but their best song is "Catch Us If You Can." It's improbably exuberant, and it's infectious. Here is its central theme: "Here they come again, mhm/Catch us if you can, mhm/Time to get a move on, mhm/We will yell with all of our might." As you might have guessed, the Dave Clark Five didn't come close to the Beatles.

If Johnson was right: *Citizen Kane* yes, *How Green Was My Valley* no; the Beatles yes, the Dave Clark Five no; Mozart yes, Salieri no; Jane Austen yes, Mary Brunton no. Johnson did not think that long-term fame could be a product of infatuation or caprice.

But recall his qualification. Those who enjoy enduring fame *owe something to us*. When someone or something becomes iconic, we fix our eyes on their graces and endure what we would despise in others.

The idea of bubbles will be central to my argument here. But Johnson got it wrong. He had nothing to say about a central question: Who gets a chance, and who does not? Who gets a break, and who does not? Who gets effective champions, and who does not? In any case, *short-term fame and long-term fame are not so different*. The intragenerational case is the intergenerational case, speeded way up; the intergenerational case is the intragenerational case, slowed way down. We cannot trust the verdict of the long term. Custom and veneration, and infatuation and caprice, make all the difference, even over centuries.

Johnson was demonstrably wrong to say that if we uncovered the long-lost work of those who were celebrated in their time, we would be disappointed in its quality, and wonder why it had once been celebrated. Much of what has been lost is very great indeed. Often we do rediscover what has been lost, and we are bowled over by it. Lightning strikes. It might strike at a surprising time—when someone who was ignored for most of their life makes it big in old age, or when a poem or a product is celebrated years after it was written or made.

We can learn large lessons from that. What's in "the canon"? Now? Twenty years from now? Fifty years from now? There are often staggering surprises.

Up Jumped the Devil

For a case in point, let's turn to another writer named Johnson—Robert, not Samuel. Have you heard of him?

A stunning guitarist and songwriter who played the blues, Johnson died in 1938.[11] He was just twenty-seven. During his short life, he was far from famous, and he made little money. Sometimes he played on street corners.[12] In his two recording sessions—and there were only two—he recorded a grand total of twenty-nine songs.[13] We know very little about his life.

In 1961, through a series of accidents, Columbia Records released an album of his songs, called *King of the Delta Blues Singers*.[14] Somehow the album caught on. Through word of mouth, it created something like a cult, which included many of the greatest popular musicians from the 1960s to the present.

Did Johnson lay the foundations for rock and roll music in its current form? Maybe.

Eric Clapton described Johnson as "the most important blues singer that ever lived."[15] Bob Dylan said that Robert Johnson's "words made my nerves quiver like piano wires."[16] Dylan reported: "The stabbing sounds from the guitar could almost break a window. When Johnson started singing, he seemed like a guy who could have sprung from the head of Zeus in full armour."[17] Dylan added, "If I hadn't heard the Robert Johnson record when I did, there probably would have been hundreds of lines of mine that would have been shut down."[18] Pause over that. It tells us something important about how culture works (art, music, literature, business, religion, politics).

Robert Johnson, so obscure in his lifetime, is now an icon. Books are written about him; documentaries are made about him.

People speculate endlessly about his mysterious life, and about how he acquired his genius. There is a legend that one day in Mississippi, Johnson went down to the crossroads—and made a deal with the devil. One of Johnson's biographies is called *Up Jumped the Devil*; another is called *Crossroads*; another is called *A Meeting at the Crossroads*.[19] From Moby, the American musician and songwriter: "For his sake I'm sorry that Robert Johnson sold his soul to the devil, but for our sake and the sake of music I'm glad he did."[20]

Johnson didn't sell his soul, of course. But it's an arresting metaphor for those who do extraordinary things. Decades after he died, Johnson was struck by lightning.

One of my main points is that there is no recipe for how to become famous, and in that sense, my title is a bit of a cheat. This is not a how-to manual. Lotteries are random draws. Consider Ecclesiastes: "The race is not to the swift, nor the battle to the strong, neither bread to the wise, nor yet riches to men of understanding, nor yet favor to men of skill; but time and chance happeneth to them all."

Let's not argue with Ecclesiastes. But as we shall see, identifiable factors matter, and they can be enlisted. Quality is important, of course. (What's quality? A good question.[21]) Tireless champions matter a lot, and they can be critical: individual advocates, managers, fans, societies, descendants, devoted children, and keepers of the flame. Johnson had Boswell; the Beatles had Brian Epstein.

The Zeitgeist can help or hurt. Sometimes it makes all the difference. Some people catch a massive wave, and for some people, there is no wave to catch. Connie Converse, on whom more later, could not find a wave. (Is she our Robert Johnson? I hope so. Too soon to tell.) An irresistible life story, full of drama and question marks, can be a spark. Mysteries are good.

Prologue

Still, what happens within one's lifetime is unpredictable, and history's verdict is fickle. Many people deliver something extraordinary but never get a chance—even the limited chance that Robert Johnson got. The tale that I will tell is one of crossroads, shifting tastes, renewal, economics, opportunity, and politics—and paths that suddenly appear, as if by magic, on the horizon.

PART ONE
Iconic

CHAPTER 1

Sliding Doors

The brilliant 2019 film *Yesterday* asks a provocative question: What would happen in a world in which the Beatles had never existed, but in which one person, by some kind of magic, knows all their songs and delivers them afresh to that world?

The hero of the film is a mediocre singer-songwriter named Jack Malik, who has failed to attract an audience, and who is giving up on his musical career. One night, there is a blackout all over the globe. When the lights go out, Malik ends up in a car accident.

Fortunately, he is not badly injured. After he is released from the hospital, he has lunch with a small group of friends, who present him with a guitar. He plays the Beatles' "Yesterday" for them. They love the song. That's hardly surprising. But bizarrely, they claim to have never heard it before. Nor, they claim, have they heard of the Beatles.

Certain that his friends must be playing some kind of joke on him, Malik goes online. He is shocked to discover that in the world in which he now lives, the Beatles are entirely unknown. Even Google knows nothing about them.

What on earth happened?

Maybe John's glamorous, adored mother, Julia, never got him a guitar? Maybe John Lennon and Paul McCartney never got together in the first place? Maybe Paul was too shy, on that fateful day in Liverpool (July 6, 1957), to introduce himself to John? Maybe John was in a sour mood and never invited Paul to join the Quarrymen, his band at the time? Maybe Julia was not hit and killed by a truck, and maybe John's life took a more conventional course, and he did not try to be a rock musician?

Maybe Paul failed to get his father's permission to go to Hamburg, where the Beatles learned how to be the Beatles? Maybe Brian Epstein, who was essential to their success, never became their manager? Maybe Epstein got discouraged and tired? Or maybe the Beatles did become a group—John, Paul, George, and Ringo—but never got a recording contract? (They nearly didn't.)

Whatever the answer, Malik immediately sees an incredible opportunity: He knows the Beatles' songs, and *no one else does*. He has a gold mine, a treasure trove. He records the songs. He performs them. He becomes a worldwide sensation.

In one of the film's most dramatic scenes, the singer-songwriter Ed Sheeran (played by himself) challenges Malik to a duel: *Who can sing the better song*? In front of a rapt audience, Sheeran delivers a terrific song. But Malik responds with "The Long and Winding Road," a Lennon-McCartney special. Sheeran immediately concedes defeat.

Much of the power of the film lies in its largely successful effort to encourage the audience to hear songs from the Beatles as if they were fresh and new—as if we were listening for the first time. What if we just heard, last night or this morning, "I Saw Her Standing There," "Let It Be," "Yesterday," "Carry That Weight," or "Here Comes the Sun"? *Yesterday* invites viewers to ask that question and in a sense to experience the answer—to discover the Beatles all over again. Because Malik becomes a worldwide phenomenon, the film depicts a version of Beatlemania without the Beatles. More subtly and equally interestingly, the film offers a clear empirical hypothesis, which it makes plausible and intuitive or perhaps irresistible: *the Beatles (I think) were surpassingly great, and their sheer greatness was, and is, a guarantee of spectacular popularity, wherever and however their music emerged.*

Would it be lovely to think so? It is hard *not* to think so. In 1966, John Lennon produced a scandal when he said, "We're more popular than Jesus now." (With respect to fame and obscurity, the full quotation is even more inflammatory, and intriguingly wrong: "Christianity will go. It will vanish and shrink. I needn't argue about that; I'm right and I'll be proved right. We're more popular than Jesus now; I don't know which will go first—rock 'n' roll or Christianity. Jesus was all right but his disciples were thick and ordinary. It's them twisting it that ruins it for me.")[1] In suggesting that Beatlemania had become akin to a religion, John captured something real about the worldwide adulation, and perhaps even worship, that the Beatles attracted at that time. See figure 1-1. (His remark also raised a question: How did Jesus get so popular, anyway? Is it illuminating to speak of Jesusmania? We'll get to that.)

With all that screaming, surely they were destined for success?

Maybe so. But in an important respect, *Yesterday* is a cheat. Many people in the audience already know the songs! We cannot unhear them. As we watch the movie unfold, we begin in a state of incredulity; we simply cannot believe that people are acting as if they have not heard, or have not even heard of, the Beatles. *Wait, what?* Who has never heard "Yesterday"?

To be sure, we can try to experience the thrill of hearing their music as if it were fresh; the movie encourages us to do that. To

Iconic

The Beatles

Source: *The Beatles at Wellington Airport*, June 20, 2013 via Creative Commons Attribution 2.0. Courtesy of Archives New Zealand Te Rua Mahara o te Kāwanatanga.

an astounding extent, it succeeds. But unlike the audiences in the film, the songs are hardly new to us. We already love them. We do not need to be introduced to them. Hence the film does not establish its central claim: because of their amazing music, the success of the Beatles, and the rise of Beatlemania, were essentially inevitable.

That claim is hard to resist, because it is comforting and orderly, and because it appeals directly to our intuitions. It does so because it offers a simple tale of causation: extraordinary work produces extraordinary rewards. In one way or another, genius is recognized. We cannot easily imagine a world in which someone replaced and outshined the Beatles—or Jane Austen, or William Wordsworth, or *Star Wars*, or Harry Potter, or Taylor Swift. Surely there are not people and things, lost to history, who really were their equivalents—who were as good as they were?

But our intuitions mislead us. In the domain of success and failure, causation is anything but simple. Clio, the goddess of history, is full of mischief. She can be beneficent. She can be cruel. She is a trickster. She has a terrific sense of humor.

A Personal Note

In 1965, I was eleven years old, walking to my school—Angier School, a public school in Waban, Massachusetts. (It still exists.) I happened to run into my best friend, whose name was Roger. Roger mentioned that he was applying to a "private school," named Rivers. (It still exists.) I didn't know what a private school was, but I was competitive, and so I asked my parents about whether I should apply too.

My mother was thrilled. My father was quiet. (I learned, decades later, that he was terrified about the expense.) My mother did a little research. A year later, she had me apply to three local schools: Belmont Hill, Noble and Greenough, and Middlesex. In public school, I had pretty good grades, but not terrific grades. I had no family connections. I was a pretty good athlete, but I was not a terrific athlete.

I interviewed badly at Belmont Hill and Noble and Greenough. How well I remember the humorless, unfriendly admissions officers at both places; they seemed to have no interest in me. At Middlesex, I was amazed by the charismatic head of admissions, Mr. Boynton, who made me laugh; I felt immediately comfortable with him. Belmont Hill and Noble and Greenough turned me down. Middlesex admitted me. I have no idea why. It seemed like a miracle.

Middlesex changed everything for me. The school taught me how to read and how to write. It taught me how to learn. It taught me how to run. There was plenty of personal attention. When I fell, a teacher would pick me up, pretending not to notice that I had fallen. Mr. Case taught me Latin. Mr. Tulp taught me about sports. Mr. Fortmiller taught me about literature and drama— Eugene Ionesco, Edward Albee, Samuel Beckett. Mr. Scott taught me French (and looked the other way, one day, when my room-mates and I may or may not have been smoking marijuana in our dorm room). Mr. Davis taught me biology. My teachers knew me; they seemed to see me.

I have had a lot of luck in life. What if I had not run into my friend Roger that day? What if my mother hadn't put Middlesex on our little list? What if Mr. Boynton hadn't liked me?

A Mistake

A number of years ago, a brilliant Harvard student—let's call her Jane—came to my office with an intriguing research project. She wanted to study the sources of success.[2] Jane's plan was to contact dozens of spectacularly successful people in multiple fields (business, politics, music, literature) and to see what they had in common. Maybe all of them had difficult childhoods. Maybe none of them had difficult childhoods. Maybe all of them were quick to anger. Maybe none of them was quick to anger. Maybe all of them developed a passion in high school. Maybe none of them developed a passion in high school. Maybe all of them were impatient. Maybe none of them was impatient.

Jane was energetic as well as astonishingly smart. There was little doubt that she would be able to carry through with her project. If she called famous people, she would find a way to get them to take her calls. Still, something was wrong with what she had in mind. Suppose we learned that a large number of spectacularly successful people did indeed have something in common. Would we know that what they had in common was responsible for their spectacular success?

Not at all. There might be plenty of people (hundreds, thousands, millions) who share that characteristic, and who did not end up spectacularly successful. The shared characteristic might not be sufficient for success. Imagine, for example, that spectacularly successful people turn out to be quick to anger. Plenty of people who are quick to anger do not succeed. Maybe they never got a chance. Maybe they got mad at the wrong person at the wrong time. Maybe they were born in poverty. Maybe they didn't have the right skin color.

If we learn that spectacularly successful people tend to be quick to anger, have we learned anything at all? Maybe not.

You might think that even if a shared characteristic is not sufficient for success, at least it is necessary for success, or contributes to success, or increases the probability of success. To be sure, you are unlikely to be impressed if you learn that all spectacularly successful people have five fingers on each hand. But you might be intrigued if the shared characteristic (say, impatience) seems to have a plausible causal relationship to success. But that's not necessarily true. It might be a coincidence, or incidental. One hundred successful people might be impatient, but is that why they became successful? Is it a contributing factor, even? How would we know?

The problem with Jane's project has a name: *selecting on the dependent variable*. Countless successful business books follow a path identical to that proposed by Jane. They try to figure out what characteristics are shared by inventors, innovators, leaders, or other successful types. If they find a shared characteristic, they urge that they have discovered a secret or clue of some kind. Maybe so. But maybe not.[3] (Probably not.)

Jim Collins's *Good to Great: Why Some Companies Make the Leap . . . and Others Don't,* for example, studies an assortment of successful companies and specifies the characteristics that they share, which include a "culture of discipline."[4] The problem is that it is possible and even likely that hundreds of companies fail even though they have a culture of discipline. I bet that you could easily find an assortment of successful companies that do not have a culture of discipline.

In Search of Excellence, by Thomas Peters and Robert Waterman, finds that forty-three successful companies show a "bias for action"—without asking whether eight hundred or eight thousand unsuccessful companies also show a bias for action.[5] (I bet eighty thousand failed companies show that bias.) Some of the most successful books on leadership single out characteristics that are shared by some number of leaders—tenacity, overcoming hardship, an ability to empathize—without asking whether those same characteristics are shared by any number of people who are terrible leaders, or not leaders at all.

Here is another way to put it. Part two of this book will focus mainly on thirteen people: William Blake, Jane Austen, John Keats, George Lucas, Bob Dylan, Stan Lee, Harry Houdini, Mina Crandon (you haven't heard of her? Okay, she was very famous once—not so much now), Ayn Rand, John Lennon, Paul McCartney, George Harrison, and Ringo Starr. We could surely find some characteristics that unify those thirteen people. And if part two of this book focused on thirty people, the same thing would be true. The difficulty is that we would have no idea whether the unifying characteristic was responsible for, or even contributed to, their fame.

Small samples are a big problem. If forty-three successful companies, or two hundred successful companies, share some characteristic, it is right to complain about the small sample size. But the most serious problem lies elsewhere. Even if we could find that eight hundred companies or two thousand companies share some characteristic, we might know very little about why they are successful.

A study of sixty-four famous scientists found that all of them showed a "driving absorption in their work."[6] OK, fine; maybe we can say that a driving absorption in one's work is necessary for scientific success. (Did we need to survey sixty-four famous scientists to know that?) But what about the sixty-four thousand not-famous scientists who also showed a driving absorption in their work?

Because so many successful books select on the dependent variable, it is tempting to say that selecting on the dependent variable is predictive of becoming a bestseller. But let us not fall into temptation.

The Power of Narratives

Why are the relevant narratives—showing that five, ten, or fifty successful companies have a certain kind of culture, or that five, ten, or fifty successful people had difficult teenage years—so convincing? Why are they hard to resist?

A mischievous research project, called "Success Stories Cause False Beliefs about Success," provides some clues.[7] George Lifchits and his colleagues asked 1,317 people to make a bet: Will a firm founded by a college dropout succeed, or will an essentially identical firm, founded by a college graduate, succeed? On which firm would you bet?

Before people made their bets, half of them were told about five successful firms with founders who dropped out of college (the college dropout condition); half were told about five successful firms with founders who did *not* drop out of college (the college graduate condition). The firms were otherwise identical. Participants in the study were informed that some people believe that companies are more likely to do exceedingly well if they are headed by a college dropout (in the college dropout condition) or a college graduate (in the college graduate condition). But participants were also told "not everyone believes that, of course," and they were informed that "there are plenty of examples" of spectacularly successful companies with founders of the opposite educational status.

After receiving this information, participants were asked a set of questions, confirming that they understood that the examples of successful companies were a biased sample. Then participants were given the choice of whether to bet on a company with a dropout founder or a college graduate founder.

The result? People's bets were greatly affected by which biased examples they were randomly assigned to see. Those who saw examples of successful companies with college graduate founders bet on the company with the college graduate founder a whopping 87 percent of the time. Those who saw examples of successful companies with dropout founders bet on the company with a college graduate founder just 32 percent of the time. This is so even though participants acknowledged selection bias in the examples they were given. And indeed, both sides reported high levels of confidence in their bets.

Participants were also given a chance to write up an account of why they decided as they did. About 99 percent did so, and many of them produced causal explanations, justifying their conclusion that the founder on whom they bet was more likely to succeed.

A majority of those who were given examples of dropout founders offered explanations of why dropout founders are likely to succeed; a majority of those who were given examples of graduate founders offered explanations of why graduate founders are likely to succeed.

What accounts for these results? The answer lies in the immense power of narratives, especially when they come with a plausible claim about causation. Suppose you hear a story about Bill Gates, founder of Microsoft. Gates was a college dropout. (He was, in fact, in my college dormitory, Currie House, at Harvard back in the 1970s. I remember him well; he was very skinny, and he really liked pinball, as did most of us, and also computers, which none of us seemed to appreciate at the time.) Learning about Gates and his astonishing success, you might well think: College dropouts have a big advantage. They have a passion. They are ahead of the game.

Now suppose you hear a tale about Jeff Bezos, founder of Amazon. Bezos is a Princeton graduate. Learning about Bezos and his astonishing success, you might well think: College graduates are of course a better bet than college dropouts. They finish what they start; they have persistence. They know what they are doing.

If the particular variable that is singled out, and on which you focus, can be intuitively associated with success, in a simple, satisfying story that your imagination helps to write, you might have to work pretty hard to see that the variable has little or no explanatory power. If you learn about successful firms that allow remote work, you might think that allowing remote work is a key to success. If you learn about successful firms that forbid remote work, you might think that forbidding remote work is a key to success.

Leonardo da Vinci's *Mona Lisa* is the most famous painting in the world. Why is that? You might want to answer that question

The Mona Lisa

Source: Mona Lisa craziness, July 19, 2009 via Creative Commons Attribution 2.0. Courtesy of Thomas van de Weerd.

by thinking long and hard about the painting and the celebrated woman in it.

You might consider her enigmatic smile. What secret is she hiding? You might ponder the way her eyes seem to follow you wherever you go. You might wonder about her folded hands. They seem to signal calm; but why, exactly, are they folded? You might emphasize the background, which is at once beautiful, dreamy, and mysterious.

The more you think about the *Mona Lisa*, the more you might admire the painting, and find it entirely unsurprising that it has achieved its iconic status. How could it not have done that? If the *Mona Lisa* were discovered today, wouldn't people be in awe, and immediately declare it one of the world's greatest masterpieces, if not the very greatest? (This is the hypothesis of *Yesterday*.)

And yet, for centuries the *Mona Lisa* was hardly the most famous painting in the world. It was widely unknown. Painted between 1503 and 1519, it was well regarded in its first decades, but it was not at all famous, and it was not seen as a masterpiece even by those who admired it. It was not until the 1860s that art critics started to like it a lot, and even at that time, it was not known to the general public. In the eighteenth and nineteenth centuries, da Vinci was not nearly as famous as he is today. The *Mona Lisa* was seen as a very good painting, not as one of the greatest paintings in the world.

How did it attain its current status? That is a long and complicated story.[8] It involves what happened *to* the painting, not what happened *in* the painting. For one thing, the *Mona Lisa* was stolen from the Louvre in 1911.[9] Without the theft, who knows whether the painting would have anything like its current status?

Charles Dickens may well be the most celebrated novelist in the English language. (If you haven't read *Great Expectations*, please do.) You might think that he has attained that status because of the unique qualities of his novels: funny, vivid, heartbreaking, sentimental, loving, poignant, quietly (and sometimes not so quietly) political. If so, you seem to be saying that Dickens is the most celebrated novelist in the English language because he is more like Dickens than anyone else. But as Duncan Watts has shown, it is circular to claim that "X succeeded because X had the attributes of X."[10] We should not say, "Taylor Swift was successful because she had exactly the attributes of Taylor Swift, and not someone else." That isn't obviously wrong, but it is not exactly an explanation.

In any case, it isn't right. There is a great deal of randomness in the world, and success and failure have everything to do with that randomness. As H. J. Jackson writes in her study of fame and Romantic literature, *Those Who Write for Immortality*, "Wordsworth, Austen,

Keats, and Blake achieved their present-day pinnacles in part or even mainly because of adventitious circumstances."[11] Adventitious circumstances mean randomness. Whether one product rises to the top, one executive becomes iconic, or one person (John F. Kennedy, Barack Obama, Donald Trump) becomes president of the United States, depends on numerous things happening to break right at the right moment. Successful politicians are like Wordsworth, Austen, Keats, and Blake, and so are corporate executives, and so are great athletes.

Eminence Studies

Some fascinating empirical work, based on massive data sets, seeks to account for "eminence" or "genius." An entire field of research is devoted to what we might call "eminence studies."[12] (There is in fact a *Journal of Genius and Eminence*, whose first volume appeared in 2016.[13]) Dean Keith Simonton of the University of California at Davis has produced many such studies. A representative finding is that intelligence matters. But how much? Summarizing an assortment of studies, Simonton concludes, "A high IQ is not irrelevant in understanding who becomes a big success."[14] That cautious statement seems unobjectionable. But Simonton adds this: "Although it is not the only factor, the higher a person's ability is, the bigger his or her impression on posterity."

That less-than-cautious statement is not sufficiently supported by the data. We might be able to find that in a data set consisting of, say, forty-five people, those with the highest IQs were the most successful. Some of the relevant studies find something like that. But any such findings prove little. We cannot know, from studies of this kind, that a high IQ is responsible for people's success—any more than we could learn much from a demonstration that the most successful people have blue eyes, small noses, or brown hair.

In one of Simonton's own studies, he explored a sample of 2,012 philosophers from AD 580 to AD 1900, asking whether identifiable factors are correlated with eminence.[15] In that study, the sample size was pretty large. He finds that philosophers are more likely to become eminent if they deal with a large number of questions rather than just a few. He also finds that extremism, rather than moderation, is correlated with eminence. Thinkers who have become eminent are more likely to be behind the times; their views are more similar to those predominant in their youth than they are to those in the next generation.

These are interesting findings, but even more interesting is the fact that after considering numerous possible contributors to eminence, Simonton finds that almost 80 percent of the variance in philosophical eminence remains unexplained! It is also reasonable to wonder whether the data actually explains that 20 percent. The significant correlations that Simonton finds—for example, between eminence and extremism—might not account for eminence, or be causally associated with it. It might be an incidental factor and not at all predictive. Consider the fact that efforts to predict cinematic success have proved exceedingly challenging, not least because of surprises that occur after release.[16]

Simonton also attempts to explain the relative popularity of Shakespeare's plays. For example, *Hamlet* and *King Lear* are toward the top, and *Timon of Athens* and *Henry VI, Part 3* are toward the bottom. He urges that identifiable factors do matter.[17] He concludes that when Shakespeare focuses on the history of the monarchy, his plays do not do so well. By contrast, plays that focus on madness or emotional excess turn out to be winners. Shakespeare's plays also do better if they deal with despotism and tyranny. That too is interesting. But what, exactly, do we learn from such findings?

Maybe Shakespeare was at his worst when writing about the history of the monarchy, and at his best when dealing with madness and despotism. (King Lear was a mad despot.) Like most people, I tend to agree that *Hamlet* and *King Lear* are Shakespeare's best, but if most people think that, we should be cautious before concluding that they really are his best, and entertain the possibility that they benefited from some kind of historical lottery. Both of them are beyond great, but to some extent, they are famous because they are famous. Are they really better than *The Tempest*, *As You Like It*, or *The Merchant of Venice*?

To be sure, it would be foolish to deny that eminence or fame might well be explained, in part, by identifiable factors of one or another kind. A great deal of attention has been paid to psychological factors in particular. No one doubts that ambition helps, and so does determination. If the Beatles gave up early, they would not have become the Beatles. Resilience helps. "Extraordinary achievement does not arise from those with lackadaisical minds," and "arduous labor" is ordinarily required.[18] Of course ability matters. George Lucas, the writer and director of *Star Wars*, is extraordinarily resilient, and he has an astounding visual imagination.

The problem is that even if we can associate certain factors with eminence, and even if we can offer some nonobvious findings, the associations tend to be fairly weak. (For example, there is a continuing dispute about whether it helps to be the first-born member of a family.) Countless people who are ambitious, determined, resilient, and able do not become eminent.[19] One more time: beware of selecting on the dependent variable!

After-the-fact claims, based on small samples or large ones, seem exceedingly plausible. They fit with our intuitions. As they say, hindsight has 20/20 vision. But to what extent is it possible to make reliable predictions about who or what will become eminent?

Stolen Bicycles

Imagine, if you would, a series of doors. If you walk through one, you will remain in the world in which you live: Leonardo da Vinci, Michelangelo, and Vincent Van Gogh are iconic artists. The Beatles and Bob Dylan are iconic musicians. Harry Potter is the hero of the most famous children's books. William Shakespeare, John Milton, and John Keats are known to be among the greatest literary figures in the English language. *Citizen Kane, The Godfather,* and the *Star Wars* films are known to rank among the greatest movies. Isabelle Huppert is known to be the world's greatest actor. (Don't argue.)

If you walk through another, you will enter a world in which all of these things are true, but no one has heard of Bob Dylan. There is another singer-songwriter, a little bit like Dylan, who seems to have taken his place; her name is Connie Converse. If you walk through another, Van Gogh, Keats, and *Star Wars* are missing, and in their stead, there are several famous artists, poets, and films that you have never heard of. And if you walk through another door, exactly none of the familiar names and titles is well-known; each of them seems to have been replaced by a name or a title that is unknown in your world.

This little exercise is, of course, a play on *Yesterday.* You might think of it as venturing the contrary hypothesis, to the effect that success and fame are not foreordained but are determined by a set of adventitious factors that happened to turn out as they did, and that could easily have turned out differently.

Iconic

Regrettably, that contrary hypothesis is exceptionally vague. What does it mean? To what factors are we pointing? If Shakespeare's parents had not been in a romantic mood on the night on which Will was conceived, there would be no Shakespeare. But perhaps that is not especially interesting?

For a period, Muhammad Ali was not only the most famous athlete on the planet. He was the most famous person. He was recognized all over the world. I met him once, in a hotel in Chicago; I was tongue-tied and barely able to tell him how much he meant to me. He was gentle, kind, and gracious. I told him a ridiculous little story about my staying up late as a young boy, to hear about the outcome of his championship fight against Sonny Liston. He acted as if that was the most interesting tale he had ever heard.

Ali was, of course, a boxer (and probably the greatest who ever lived). How did he get into boxing? When he was just twelve years old and named Cassius Marcellus Clay Jr., he had a red bicycle, which he dearly loved. One day that bicycle was stolen. Young Clay reported the theft to Joe Martin, a police officer in Louisville, Kentucky. Clay told Martin that he wanted to "whup" the thief.

As it happened, Martin ran Columbia Gym on South Fourth Street in Louisville, and told Clay that if he wanted to "whup" someone, he should learn to box. That's where it all started. What would have happened if the thief had not stolen Clay's bicycle? What would have happened if Clay had reported the theft to some other police officer?

True, we have to draw some distinctions. Great athletes are different from great musicians; great writers are different from great politicians; great business leaders are not the same as great scientists. In some cases, we have objective measures of success. Ali beat Sonny Liston and George Foreman in the ring; Usain Bolt could run faster than anyone else in the world; in her prime, Serena

Williams was the best tennis player in the world. There isn't a lot of debate about those propositions.

In the arts, we might lack a consensus. I think that Stephen King is very great indeed; in my view, he is our Charles Dickens. But I have to acknowledge that many people disagree, and that I cannot easily prove that they are wrong. Business and politics are complicated cases. Steve Jobs made a lot of money. Franklin Delano Roosevelt was elected president—four times. Both of them were amazing. And how did people like that get where they got? There is no single answer to that question.

Still: across diverse domains, there are commonalities. At some point in their lives, some people meet someone who gets them interested in something new, or who cultivates their talents. If they had not met that person, they might not have become iconic. Some people have extraordinary talents, and cultivate them, but to succeed, they badly need some kind of additional support—a school, a spouse, a partner, a manager, a sponsor, an organizer who might have started as a mere fan. Some people need to be attached, or need to get attached, to the temper or mood of the nation or the time. They can be spectacularly successful in one decade; but they would have failed abysmally, or been found incomprehensible, in a previous decade, and in a future decade they would have seemed outmoded.

On September 29, 1961, Robert Shelton gave a rave review in the *New York Times* to a complete unknown: twenty-year-old Bob Dylan. Shelton wrote:

Resembling a cross between a choir boy and a beatnik, Mr. Dylan has a cherubic look and a mop of tousled hair he partly covers with a Huck Finn black corduroy cap. His clothes may need a bit of tailoring, but when he works his guitar, harmonica or piano and composes new songs faster than he can remember them, there is no doubt that he is bursting at the seams with talent. Mr. Dylan's voice is anything but pretty. He is consciously trying to recapture the rude beauty of a Southern field hand musing in melody on his porch. All the "husk and bark" are left on his notes and a searing intensity pervades his songs. . . . Mr. Dylan is vague about his antecedents and birthplace, but it matters less where he has been than where he is going, and that would seem to be straight up.[20]

Shelton's review helped to launch Dylan's career. Would Dylan have taken off if Shelton had decided to write about someone else? Someone who was really good, whom you've never heard of?

Keynes

John Maynard Keynes was, and is, very famous, but let's put his fame to one side, and focus on one of his interests: the limits of prediction. Keynes's analysis bears directly on the question of whether and when we can predict success or failure.

Keynes enthusiastically agreed that many things could be predicted well enough, but he drew attention as well to the problem of "uncertainty," which arises when we cannot assign probabilities to outcomes. Consider these remarks:

> By "uncertain" knowledge, let me explain, I do not mean merely to distinguish what is known for certain from what is only probable. The game of roulette is not subject, in this sense, to uncertainty; nor is the prospect of a Victory bond being drawn. Or, again, the expectation of life is only slightly

uncertain. Even the weather is only moderately uncertain. The sense in which I am using the term is that in which the pros-pect of a European war is uncertain, or the price of copper and the rate of interest twenty years hence, or the obsolescence of a new invention, or the position of private wealth-owners in the social system in 1970. About these matters there is no scientific basis on which to form any calculable probability whatever.[21]

Hence Keynes's punchline: "We simply do not know."

Keynes acknowledged that people have time-honored strate-gies for handling such situations. For example: "We assume that the present is a much more serviceable guide to the future than a candid examination of past experience would show it to have been hitherto. In other words, we largely ignore the prospect of future changes about the actual character of which we know nothing."[22]

Alternatively: "Knowing that our own individual judgment is worthless, we endeavor to fall back on the judgment of the rest of the world, which is perhaps better informed. That is, we endeavor to conform to the behavior of the majority or the average. The psy-chology of a society of individuals each of whom is endeavoring to copy the others leads to what we may strictly term a conventional judgment."[23]

Both of these techniques were, and remain, pervasive in both business and politics. In deciding how to handle a national secu-rity crisis, many officials ask: How were similar national crises handled in the past? In deciding how to handle climate change, many companies ask: What are other companies doing?

But Keynes did not mean to celebrate such techniques. On the contrary, he thought that they were ridiculous. "All these pretty, polite techniques, made for a well-panelled Board Room and a nicely regulated market, are liable to collapse," because "we know very little about the future."[24]

Life Trajectories

In 2020, a large team of researchers—112, to be exact—engaged in an unusually ambitious project. They wanted to see if life trajectories could be predicted. To do that, they challenged the world. Their challenge had a simple name: the Fragile Families Challenge.[25]

The challenge began with an extraordinary data set, known as the Fragile Families and Child Wellbeing Study, which was specifically created in order to enable social science research. That study, which is ongoing, offers massive amounts of data about thousands of families, all with unmarried parents. Each of the mothers gave birth to a child in a large city in the United States around 2000.

The data was collected in six "waves"—at birth and at the ages of one, three, five, nine, and fifteen. Each collection produced a great deal of information, involving child health and development, demographic characteristics, education, income, employment, relationships with extended kin, father-mother relationships, and much more. Some of the data was collected by asking a battery of questions to both the mother and the father. Some of it came from an in-home assessment (at ages three, five, and nine) that included measurements of height and weight, observations of the neighborhood and home, and various tests of vocabulary and reading comprehension. The Fragile Families Challenge was initially launched when data had been collected from the first five waves (from birth to the age of nine years), but when complete data from the sixth wave (year fifteen) was not yet available.

That was a terrific advantage, because it allowed the researchers to create the challenge, which was to predict the following outcomes:

1. Child grade point average

2. Child grit (determined by a self-reported measure that includes perseverance)

3. Household eviction

4. Household material hardship

5. Layoff of the primary caregiver

6. Participation in job training by the primary caregiver

Those who took the challenge were given access to background material from the first five waves, and also to data on one-half of the families from the sixth wave. The material contained data on a total of 4,262 families, with a whopping 12,942 variables about each family. The central task was to build a model, based on the data that was available, that would predict outcomes for those families, during the sixth wave, for whom data was not available.

The researchers sought to recruit a large number of participants in the Fragile Families Challenge. They succeeded. In the end, they received 457 initial applications, which were winnowed down to 160 teams. Many of the teams used state-of-the-art machine-learning methods, explicitly designed to increase accuracy. The central question was simple: Which of the 160 teams would make good predictions?

The answer is: none of them!

True, the machine-learning algorithms were better than random; they were not horrible. But they were not a lot better than random, and for single-event outcomes—such as whether the primary caregiver had been laid off or had been in job training—they were only *slightly* better than random. The researchers conclude that "low predictive accuracy cannot easily be attributed to the limitations of any particular researcher or approach; hundreds of researchers attempted the task, and none could predict accurately."[26]

Notwithstanding their diverse methods, the 160 teams produced predictions that were pretty close to one another—and not so good. As the researchers slyly put it, "the submissions were much better at predicting each other than at predicting the truth."[27]

A reasonable lesson is that we really do not understand the relationship between where families are in one year and where they will be a few years hence. Seeming to draw that lesson, the authors of the Fragile Families Challenge suggest that their results "raise questions about the absolute level of predictive performance that is possible for some life outcomes, even with a rich data set."[28] You can learn a great deal about where someone now is in life, and still, you might not be able to say very much at all about specific outcomes in the future.

Tank Man

Here is a way to understand that point. Take a girl who is ten years old and learn everything you can about her: her family, her demographics, her neighborhood, her schooling, her sports. Now predict various things about her life at the age of twenty-one. Do you have much confidence in your prediction?

You shouldn't. The number of variables that can move a life in one direction or another is very high, and it is not possible to foresee them in advance. Someone might break a leg at a crucial moment, meet an amazing music teacher, find a new friend, hear a song on the radio on Sunday morning, or see something online or on the news that changes everything.

Speaking of which: I know a woman who was intensely focused on sports in both high school and college. She loved basketball and baseball in particular. She did not have clear career plans. She hoped to be a sports announcer. As a college student in 1989, she was working for a television network in Atlanta during a baseball broadcast, and she happened to see the feed of the horrifying events in Tiananmen Square, China. In particular, she saw an unidentified man, known as Tank Man, who stood in front of a set of tanks.

The young woman was riveted by what she saw. She decided to refocus her life. She started to study politics and history, and to focus more intensely on her studies. After college, she became a war correspondent. She went to law school, where she wrote a book on genocide, which won the Pulitzer Prize.

Soon after he was elected, a young senator named Barack Obama read that book, liked it, invited her to dinner, and befriended her. When he was elected president, Obama asked her to work in the White House as his human rights adviser. She became the youngest United States Ambassador to the United Nations. As I write, she is the Administrator of the United States Agency for International Development, the largest development agency in the world.

Her name is Samantha Power. She is my wife.

CHAPTER 2

Shocks and Surprises

C onnie Converse is widely known, of course, as the most original, and perhaps the greatest, of the folk singers of the 1950s and 1960s. Described as "the first singer-songwriter," she is often ranked with Bob Dylan, whom she preceded. She greatly influenced not only Dylan, but also Joan Baez, Joni Mitchell, Judy Collins, the Beatles, the Rolling Stones, James Taylor, Cat Stevens, and Crosby, Stills, Nash, and Young—and more recently, Aimee Mann, Beyoncé, Kanye West, and Taylor Swift.

You undoubtedly know one of her greatest hits, "Roving Woman," whose defiant sensibility defined an era, and which can be heard on the radio even today. A glimpse:

> People say a roving woman
> Is likely not to be better than she ought to be;
> So, when I stray away from where I've got to be,
> Someone always takes me home. . . .

Of course, there's bound to be some little aftermath
That makes a pleasant ending for the straight and narrow path.
And as I go to sleep, I cannot help but think
How glad I am that I was saved from cards and drink.

In the 1950s, people were both scandalized and delighted by the sexy mischief here. And of course, the song's meaning is much debated. Is it a feminist anthem, or just the opposite? What exactly is Converse saying about men? Is she fond of them? Is she contemptuous?

In academic circles, Converse's song is generally believed to be an ironic, upbeat celebration of female agency—something that presaged certain forms of feminism today. (Consider here Beyoncé's off-the-charts admiration for Converse.) It is agreed that "Roving Woman" is much subtler, and more interesting, than Helen Reddy's "I Am Woman/Hear Me Roar," though Reddy claims to have been directly inspired by Converse, and to have written her own anthem in direct, hard-hitting response to Converse's very different one.

You almost certainly know Converse's haunting, mournful "One by One," that aching tale of loneliness and alienation:

We go walking in the dark.
We go walking out at night.

And it's not as lovers go,
Two by two, to and fro;
But it's one by one—
One by one in the dark.

"One by One" has mystery at its core. Is it about lost love? Or a love that was desperately hoped for, but that never was? Is it a plea? An attempted seduction? A love letter? Whatever else it is, it is surely a deliberate play on the end of *Paradise Lost* and hence on the Fall: "They hand in hand with wandring steps and slow/ Through Eden took thir solitarie way."

Converse is not only a pioneering folk singer. When she "went electric," in 1965, she and Dylan built the foundations of modern rock music. On this, she followed Dylan by a few months, though she preceded him in writing new folk songs. She is often taught in literature courses, and some people believe that in the fullness of time, a Nobel Prize is not out of the question.

"Dozens of Fans All over the World"

Okay, okay, I have been lying; I described a counterfactual world. But some of what I have just said is true, and the world I described is not entirely counterfactual. Connie Converse was indeed a folk singer in the 1950s. "Roving Woman" and "One by One" are real songs, and Converse wrote them, but she never released a commercial album. She never played to a large audience. She had no hits. She played mostly to friends and family. (In fact, it would be excessive to say that she played to "audiences.") Converse tried hard to make it, and she did attract some interest from well-connected people, some of whom tried to help her. But she was never "discovered."

As she put it, "I have dozens of fans all over the world." That is the same sensibility that produced the mischievous, double-take–producing line, "People say a roving woman/Is likely not to be better than she ought to be."

Startlingly, Converse appeared on national television—but just once, with Walter Cronkite. There is no video or audio recording of her appearance (only photographs), and the appearance did not give her career any kind of boost. She was writing folk songs before people wrote folk songs. She didn't fit in any kind of niche. Was she a genius? Was she a victim of discrimination? What kind of discrimination? Was she before her time?

Frustrated by a decade of failure, she essentially stopped writing music in the late 1950s. In 1961, she moved from New York to Ann Arbor, Michigan, where she became managing editor of an academic journal. She left New York in the very same month that Bob Dylan arrived there. Apparently he never heard of her. (He did a bit better than she did.) She disappeared in 1974, at the age of fifty, when she left her home in Ann Arbor, in her Volkswagen Beetle. She wrote a number of opaque goodbye notes to friends and family, saying that she was returning to New York.

No one knows where she went, or what happened to her. It is generally believed that she committed suicide. Neither her body nor her car was ever found. It is all a mystery.

But that is not the end of the story. Not close. On January 9, 2004, Gene Deitch, a famous cartoonist who was also an amateur recording engineer, was asked to appear on a radio show in New York—WYNC's *Spinning on Air,* hosted by David Garland. Eighty years old, Deitch had a lot of recordings. He sent a sample of what he had to Garland, who did not much like what he heard. But there was an exception: Garland loved Connie Converse.

It turned out that when living in New York in the 1950s, Deitch had used a new tape recorder to capture the music of his guests at various small, informal gatherings he would organize. At one such gathering in 1954, Deitch recorded Converse. He told Garland that he had been stunned by what he heard, but that he failed to stay in touch with her, and that she had disappeared in the 1970s.

Intrigued by the tale, Garland asked Deitch to talk on air about the mysterious Converse, and also to play some of her music. Deitch chose "One by One." He claimed that in 1954, those at his small gathering had fallen "in love with her music" and that Converse was a "lost genius." He spoke about her for about a minute.

That might have been the end of the matter. In a logical world, it probably ought to have been. But as it happened, Dan Dzula, a twenty-year-old college student in New York, was listening to that very episode of *Spinning on Air* while driving to his parents' house on a Sunday night. He was knocked out by what he heard. He absorbed "One by One" in stunned silence. As soon as he got home, Dzula tried to find out everything he could about Converse. What he found online was: nothing at all. Puzzled and rapt, he replayed the episode of *Spinning on Air* and recorded, just for himself, Converse's rendition of "One by One."

After graduating from college, Dzula began work at a studio as an engineer, mixing and producing. He asked his college classmate, David Herman, to join him there. All the while, he continued to be intrigued by Converse and would occasionally play "One by One" for his friends. Again: in a logical world, that might also have been the end of matter. But on one afternoon, Dzula played the song for Herman, who immediately saw an opportunity: Shouldn't the two of them try to find Converse's songs? Shouldn't they compile and release a debut album, more than a half-century after her death?

In 2007, Dzula wrote Deitch, volunteering to try to do exactly that. Deitch immediately sent a package to Dzula the next day, with seventeen songs by Converse. Dzula also engaged Converse's family, and her brother, the distinguished political scientist Philip Converse, was able to provide him with a number of recordings. In late 2008, Dzula and Herman decided to release Converse's music commercially.

They began with a digital EP, consisting of only three songs. They posted a link to it on social media, alongside a short account of Converse's life. The reaction was spectacular. Encouraged, they produced a full-length album, *How Sad, How Lovely,* in 2009. Garland devoted an entire episode to Converse. The album has turned out to be a huge success. As of 2023, the album has been streamed on Spotify more than 16 million times.

Converse isn't quite in the canon of folk music, but she is getting there. If she does, it might be because of Howard Fishman's riveting book on Converse, *To Anyone Who Ever Asks,* which was published in 2023.[1] Fishman happened to hear a song of hers—from *How Sad, How Lovely*—at a party in 2010, and he has been focused on her ever since. His book is a love letter, a lament, and an effort to correct what he sees as a shocking injustice.

In Fishman's account, Converse really was a genius, and she should have been recognized as such in her time. Fishman quotes Ellen Stekert, a scholar of folk music: "She was the female Bob Dylan. She was even better than him, as a lyricist and composer, but she didn't have his showbiz savvy, and she wasn't interested in writing protest songs."[2] Fishman says something similar, pointing to the role of serendipity: "Dylan was in the right place at the right time. Converse was not."[3]

Stekert's statement is too strong. Converse was not the female Bob Dylan, and she was certainly not better than he was. Still, she was original, and she was poetic. She was heartbreaking, and she was funny. She visited the depths. She was much more complicated, and much more surprising, than Joan Baez or Judy Collins. Both of them were and are both great and amazing, but Converse was more original and in important ways better. It is easy to imagine a counterfactual world in which she really did define her era. In that sense, Fishman had it just right.

Why had no one heard of her until 2008? In short: She lost the lottery. Fishman quotes her brother as saying, "Sis did not miss the

Big Time by a whole lot." Fishman himself thinks that Converse "was anything *but* lucky."[4] Her appearance with Walter Cronkite "was almost the lucky break she needed. Almost."[5] He argues that Converse had a deficit of one thing above all: connections. Here's how he ends his book: "My hope is that I have somehow at least served as a worthy shepherd, and that others will follow along, joining in the parade behind Converse as she makes her way at last to the place she belongs, to the table of great American artists and thinkers."[6]

Fishman also has something to ask: "How many Connie Converses are there out there—marginalized talents waiting to be heard; artists and thinkers lacking the emotional tools, the encouragement, the self-esteem, the community, needed to thrive?"[7]

Trapped in an Orange Peel

A number of years ago, three social scientists—Matthew Salganik, Duncan Watts, and Peter Dodds—investigated the sources of cultural success and failure.[8] Their starting point was that those who sell books, movies, television shows, and songs often have a great deal of trouble predicting what will succeed. Even experts make serious mistakes. Some products are far more successful than anticipated, whereas others are far less so. This seems to suggest, very simply, that those that succeed must be far better than those that do not. But if they are so much better, why are predictions so difficult?

We know that a new book by Stephen King is likely to do well; we know that a new song by Taylor Swift is likely to be a hit. We know that a horrible book or a horrible song is probably doomed. But there doesn't appear to be a lot more that we know. Who knew that a 2009 album by Connie Converse, a singer who disappeared decades before, would go viral on Spotify?

To explore the sources of cultural success and failure, Salganik and his coauthors created an artificial music market on a preexisting website. The result is often called the Music Lab experiment. In their experiment, the site offered people an opportunity to hear forty-eight real but unknown songs by real but unknown bands. One song, by a band called Calefaction, was "Trapped in an Orange Peel." Another, by Hydraulic Sandwich, was "Separation Anxiety." Another song, by Silverfox, was "Gnaw." Another, by Fading Through, was "Wish Me Luck." (An especially good title for purposes of this book.) Another, by Salute the Dawn, was "I Am Error." (Also good for our purposes.)

The experimenters randomly sorted half of about fourteen thousand site visitors into an "independent judgment" group, in which they were invited to listen to brief excerpts, to rate songs, and to decide whether to download them. From those seven thousand visitors, Salganik and his coauthors could obtain a clear sense of what people liked best. The other seven thousand visitors were sorted into a "social influence" group, which was exactly the same except in just one respect: people in the social influence group could see how many times each song had been downloaded by other participants.

Those in the social influence group were also randomly assigned to one of eight subgroups, *in which they could see only the number of downloads in their own subgroup.* In those different subgroups, it was inevitable that different songs would attract different initial numbers of downloads as a result of serendipitous or random factors. For example, "Trapped in an Orange Peel" might attract strong support from the first listeners in one subgroup, whereas it might attract no such support in another. "Wish Me Luck" might be unpopular in its first hours in one subgroup but attract a great deal of favorable attention in another. For vividness, we might think of the experiment as testing the potential success or failure of Cliff Richard and the Shadows, Rory Storm and the Hurricanes, Freddie and the Dreamers, the Honeycombs, and the Swinging Blue Jeans—bands from the 1960s that are not exactly famous today—and as comparing their potential success, in real time, to that of the Beatles and the Rolling Stones.

The research questions were simple. Would the eight subgroups differ in their rankings? Would the initial numbers affect where songs would end up in terms of total number of downloads? Would the initial numbers affect the ultimate rankings of the forty-eight songs?

You might hypothesize that after a period, quality would always prevail—that in this relatively simple setting, where various extraneous factors (such as reviews, energetic managers, radio placements, concerts, and word of mouth) were not at work, the popularity of the songs, as measured by their download rankings, would be roughly the same in the independent group and in all eight of the social influence groups. (Recall that for purposes of the experiment, quality is being measured solely by reference to what happened within the control group.)

It's a tempting hypothesis, but that is not at all what happened. "Wish Me Luck" could be a major hit or a miserable flop, depending on whether a lot of other people initially downloaded it and were seen to have done so. To a significant degree, everything turned on initial popularity. Almost any song could end up popular or not, depending on whether or not the first visitors liked it.

Importantly, there is one qualification to which I will return: the songs that did the very best in the independent judgment group rarely did very badly, and the songs that did the very worst in the independent judgment group rarely did spectacularly well. But otherwise, *almost anything could happen.*

The apparent lesson, consistent with Keynes's strictures and with what we have seen thus far, is that success and failure are exceedingly hard to predict. There are many reasons. Here is just one: It is difficult to know, in advance, whether a product (or a person) will benefit from the equivalent of early downloads. It is difficult to know that because so much depends on a large number of factors, some of them random. Who happens to be in a good mood, and who happens to be in a bad mood? Who wants to listen to a song? Who wants to buy a product? Who happens to have free moments at a relevant time? What is the weather at relevant times? Is it cold? Is it snowing? Is it hot?

Think a moment about what city you are in right now, or the block on which you live, and what job you have, or who your partner is, and whether or not you have one. Might one or more of those also be a product of random factors? We might ask similar questions about famous singers, executives, poets, and politicians, and about history's iconic figures.

The Music Lab Is Everywhere

The same lessons emerge from other experiments, building on what happened in the Music Lab.[9] It is not exactly news to say that in the United States, Republicans and Democrats disagree on a lot of questions. But suppose you identify a set of political proposals and ideas, and sort people into groups in which they can see what proposals and ideas are getting early support, in real time, from Republicans or Democrats. The idea might be "genetically modified food should be labeled," or "nanotechnology should be heavily regulated."

You might think that Republicans and Democrats will be influenced by what they see as the merits of the idea and their ideologies—not by whether a proposal or an idea gets early support from one or another side. If so, you would be wrong.[10]

Ideas are like songs. Suppose that in one subgroup, the early Republicans endorse an idea. If so, other Republicans will be likely to endorse it too, and Democrats will be likely to reject it. After a while, Republicans might overwhelmingly endorse it and Democrats might overwhelmingly reject it—*only because the early Republicans happened to endorse it.* Precisely the opposite can happen in another subgroup if the early Democrats endorse the same idea; in that subgroup, Democrats will end up loving the idea, and Republicans will end up hating it, only because the early Democrats happened to endorse it.

If this seems artificial, consider the fact that on many issues, Republicans and Democrats do indeed switch sides over the years, depending on what prominent leaders say and think. In recent years, Republicans have not been enthusiastic about immigration and have opposed efforts to control climate change; they thought exactly the opposite not so long ago. We can find similar things in many nations, where people take cues from what others like them seem to think—and where what others like them seem to think can be a product of random factors, such as whether a prominent leader happens to go in one direction rather than another at a critical moment.

Of course there are limits. If you oppose abortion on principle, you are not likely to start to approve of the right to choose merely because prominent people in your political party start to do that. If you do not like capital punishment, you might stand firm in your convictions even if your favorite politicians come out in favor of capital punishment. But across a wide range of issues, people do not have strong convictions, and they take cues from people whom they trust.

What about business? What about products? Where do people want to travel? Where do people want to study? What objects do people like or not like? With respect to products, an experiment modeled on the Music Lab found the same pattern.[11] The experiment involved "Meet the Ganimals," an online platform where people can generate and curate "ganimals," which are AI-generated hybrid animals. People can also say how much they like particular ganimals and rate them in terms of cuteness, creepiness, realism, and other variables.

As in the Music Lab experiment, people were sorted into (1) groups in independent conditions, in which they made evaluations entirely on their own and (2) groups in social influence conditions, in which they could see what other people thought. Just as in the Music Lab experiment, participants in the social influence conditions were randomly assigned to one of multiple online "worlds," each of which evolved independently of the others. Participants saw only ganimals discovered and votes cast by others in their

Some Ganimals

Source: Used by permission of Ziv Epstein (MIT Media Lab).

online world, and the ranking of ganimals was based only on votes in that world.

You might think that some ganimals really are adorable and that others really are not, and that in the end, the adorable ones would be counted as adorable, and the not-adorable ones would be counted as not-adorable. But here again, social influences greatly mattered. In the social influence worlds, outcomes turned out to highly unpredictable. Without social influences, different groups converged in their enthusiasm toward precisely the same set of ganimal features. (If you are curious: ganimals with eyes, a head, and doglike features.) But with social influences, groups rapidly evolved into diverse local cultures that dramatically diverged from those in the independent judgment conditions. One ganimal could be spectacularly popular in one group and not at all popular in another. The findings were very similar to those in the Music Lab.

Shall we draw a large lesson? Many markets have a lot in common with the market for ganimals. Of course intrinsic quality matters. People aren't going to think that a gruesome ganimal is adorable. If you have something with eyes, a head, and doglike features, you might be golden. But maybe not. Diverse local cultures can arise, and a fabulous product might get attention in one of them, and no attention at all in another. The iPhone has about 66 percent of the market in Japan, and less than 20 percent of the market in Brazil.[12]

Perspective

For perspective, consider a tempting view, consistent with *Yesterday: Because of their quality, some cultural products— whether music, art, novels, poetry, or ganimals—are genuinely destined for success, while others are unquestionably doomed to failure.* The Beatles' songs were in the first category; Synergy's songs were in the second. (In case you don't know, Synergy was an early-1970s rock group for which I was the drummer; we were pathetic. We did a few school dances. We weren't discovered. No one liked us.)

But before accepting that view, it is fair to ask: What, exactly, does the italicized sentence in the previous paragraph mean? Let us simply suggest that we are really speaking of probabilities. Roughly: if history could be run ten thousand times, and if there were significant variations in each, success would happen, for some cultural products, almost all of the time, and failure would occur, for some cultural products, essentially all of the time. But that apparent clarification raises many questions of its own. What are "significant variations?" What makes them significant? How many of them are there, and how do they interact with each other? If history is being rerun, what precisely are we changing, and what are we holding constant? We could rerun history one hundred thousand times, or 10 million times, but what is history looking like, each time?

Let us venture, then, a more intelligible, more specific, and more cautious claim: If a song, a painting, a novel, a poem, a movie, or a product is truly sensational, it will almost certainly be recognized as such, and if a song, a painting, a novel, a poem, a movie, or a product is truly terrible, it will disappear. The Beatles, Bob Dylan, Taylor Swift, Charles Dickens, Thomas Hardy, John Keats, and the MacBook Air were essentially bound for success simply because of their quality. Recall that the songs that did the very best in the independent judgment group rarely did very badly. And if a song, a novel, a poem, or a ganimal is horrible, it will not do well. (Of course, we would need to specify the criteria for a conclusion that something is sensational or horrible; let us simply make a stipulation here.) But within a wide range, people and products of all kinds can do very well or very poorly, and within that range (back to Keynes), predictions are hazardous.

For music (and much else), a great deal would seem to depend on social influences, which could go in all sorts of directions. We could have *multiple equilibria*: social situations or outcomes that are stable, and that are different from one another, depending on initial conditions.

But in light of what happened in the Music Lab, even this view, while intuitively plausible, is far too cautious about the role of social influences, and far too confident about the role of quality. To be sure, terrible songs, terrible works of literature, and terrible laptops are unlikely to succeed (with occasional horrifying exceptions). Sad but true: Synergy could not possibly have done well. But the best ones are hardly destined for success. Connie Converse was one of the best ones (I think), and so was Robert Johnson (for sure). After all, the Music Lab experiment itself was tightly controlled. It tested only forty-eight songs. In real markets there are countless more. And in those real-world markets, media attention, critical acclaim, marketing, product placement, champions, timing, and sheer luck (understood as a constellation of random factors) play a significant role.

How many Converses and Johnsons have you never heard of? Perhaps they never got a chance to record anything at all. Perhaps they made some recordings, now lost in someone's basement.

Social influences can be understood very broadly, and if so, they include much more than early downloads. Did an influential person endorse a product at just the right time? Did someone write something about the product in the *Wall Street Journal* or the *New York Times*? And the universe of contingency includes much more than social influences. Who even got started? Who was even in a position to get started? Who is in what kind of mood when? Who is busy, and who has time on their hands? What is the weather like? Who is having a tough time with their spouse or their child? Whose sports team won the day before?

With these points in mind, suppose that in an experimental setting, "Wish Me Luck" almost always does well and "Separation Anxiety" almost never does. It does not follow that if "Wish Me Luck" is released to the public, the song will be a large success, or that "Separation Anxiety" will fail. At least above a certain threshold of quality, everything might turn out to depend on the range of social influences, and other factors, that come into play after the release. As we will see, a conclusion of that general sort holds for the writers of the Romantic period, and if it holds for those writers, it is likely to hold very broadly.

There are larger points. Why does a writer end up writing? Why does an innovator end up innovating? Why did Steve Jobs end up where he did? Who was essential to his success, and how did Jobs encounter that essential person, or those essential people?

You have probably heard of Fleetwood Mac, one of the most beloved and successful rock bands in history. Their album *Rumours* has sold over 40 million copies; it is one of the twelve best-selling albums of all time.[13] The band's most famous members are Stevie Nicks and Lindsey Buckingham. Founded in 1967 by drummer Mick Fleetwood, Fleetwood Mac originally had neither Nicks nor Buckingham; it was a blues band, and it was not successful.[14] In 1974, Fleetwood just happened to hear a tape of Nicks and Buckingham, who were in their own group, imaginatively named Buckingham/Nicks. Fleetwood was trying out a new studio, Sound City in Los Angeles, and the engineer happened to play that particular tape for Fleetwood just to show him how the studio sounded.[15]

A week later, Bob Welch, one of the group's guitarists, left Fleetwood Mac, which meant that the group needed a new guitar player.[16] Fleetwood immediately asked Buckingham to join, and Buckingham said that he would do so only if Nicks could join too.[17] As they say, the rest is history. What if the obscure engineer had not played that tape?

Sugar Man

Consider a tale told in 2012, when the Oscar for Best Documentary was awarded to *Searching for Sugar Man*.[18] The film focuses on an unsuccessful Detroit singer-songwriter named Sixto Rodriguez, also known as Sugar Man, who released two albums in the early 1970s. Almost no one bought his albums, and his label dropped him. Not surprisingly, Rodriguez stopped making records and sought work as a demolition man. His two albums were forgotten. A family man with three daughters, Rodriguez was hardly miserable. But working in demolition, he struggled.

The film suggests that having abandoned his musical career, Rodriguez had no idea that he had become a spectacular success in South Africa—a giant, a legend, comparable to the Beatles, Bob Dylan, and the Rolling Stones. People said his name slowly and with awe, even reverence: "Rodriguez." Describing him as "the soundtrack to our lives," South Africans bought hundreds of thousands of copies of his albums, starting in the 1970s.

His South African fans speculated about his mysterious departure from the musical scene. Why did he suddenly stop making records? According to one rumor, he burned himself to death onstage. *Searching for Sugar Man* is about the contrast between the failed career of Detroit's obscure demolition man and the renown of South Africa's mysterious rock icon.

The film is easily taken as a real-world fairy tale and barely believable. It does not attempt to give an explanation for the contrast between Rodriguez's general failure and his extraordinary success in South Africa. We might be tempted to think that (for example) his music resonated with the South African culture. Perhaps so. It might seem plausible to speculate that in a period of racial division and cultural upheaval, there was something about Rodriguez that connected deeply with South Africa. We will get to such explanations in due course. But an alternative explanation is that *Searching for Sugar Man* depicts a real-life version of the Music Lab experiment. Perhaps Rodriguez found himself in numerous counterfactual worlds, and because of an absence of early downloads in most, he was forgotten in nearly all of them. But in one, early downloads were numerous, and he became an icon.

We can see Rodriguez as analogous to Robert Johnson and Connie Converse. With Rodriguez, success and failure were across space: spectacular fame in South Africa (and also Australia, as it happens), and ignoble failure everywhere else. With Johnson and Converse, success and failure were across time: spectacular fame decades after their deaths, and ignoble failure during their lifetimes. But whether we are speaking of space or time, the underlying sources of success and failure are essentially the same.

Or consider the saga of *The Cuckoo's Calling*, a crackling detective novel with a big heart, published in 2013 by an unknown author, Robert Galbraith. The novel got some excellent reviews, but it didn't sell well. A critical success but a commercial failure, it looked as if it would join the ranks of the many literary

Rodriguez types—excellent, maybe even better than that, but unable to hit the big time. Maybe Galbraith would quit writing and become a demolition man. After a while, however, a little information was released to the public: "Robert Galbraith" was, and is, J. K. Rowling!

In short order, *The Cuckoo's Calling* vaulted to the bestseller list.[19] It deserved it, but it couldn't possibly have gotten there without the magic of Rowling's name. Of course, that's not quite the Music Lab. *The Cuckoo's Calling* didn't bust out because early adopters liked it. But it's similar. Whatever its quality, the novel needed some kind of social boost, and that magical name did the trick. (Note also that if the novel had been terrible, it would have struggled, even with the name; quality was necessary.) Galbraith/Rowling followed *The Cuckoo's Calling* with a series of other novels featuring the same lead character. They're terrific, and they deserve their large audiences. But they also were big hits, as they wouldn't have been without Rowling's name. A name can be the equivalent of a large number of early downloads, and then the Matthew Effect starts to kick in. We'll get to that in chapter 3.

A Very Quick Note on Modern Technologies

Social influences are not exactly new. They played a large role in a famous two-person society in the Garden of Eden, and they are a hope and a concern for every religious tradition. Something like the Music Lab helps account for fame in the first century and the fifth, and the tenth century and the twenty-first, and every century in between. As we will see, the rise of religious and political leaders, and of canons of multiple sorts, has a great deal to do with social influences. Still, the Music Lab and analogous experiments occurred online, and it is natural to wonder whether something like surprising fame, and multiple equilibria, are more likely now than ever before.

Instant celebrity, or something like that, is with us more than at any point in human history. Could the Kardashians have become so famous a hundred years ago? What, exactly, are they famous for? Think for the moment about TikTok, YouTube, Facebook, and analogues or successors that are barely on the horizon.

A lot could be said about this question, but I am not going to say a lot about it here. At the same time, it is worth underlining the obvious point that online, it is staggeringly easy to generate social influences, by triggering either the appearance or the reality of widespread enthusiasm in essentially an instant. On a social media site, for example, a day or an hour might vault some person or product into real prominence, not least by giving people an immediate sense that that person or that product is liked or admired by many other people—and perhaps that money is changing hands in return for, say, a song, a work of art, a memento, or a book. Despite countless predecessors and analogues, the Music Lab itself could not, of course, have been created without the internet.

It follows that the sheer acceleration of fame and famousness is something new, and as they say, we ain't seen nothin' yet. Still, the central mechanisms, my next topic, are as old as humanity itself. They are the foundations for today's accelerations, and for tomorrow's too.

CHAPTER 3

Magic

You are probably familiar with a bell curve, depicting a "normal distribution" or a "Gaussian distribution." Figure 3-1 is an example.

In a normal distribution, the mean, the median, and the mode are the same. Human height is normally distributed. The mean, or average, is at the top (in the United States, around five feet nine), and measurements are symmetrical around the mean. Birth weight is also normally distributed. Other examples of normal distributions in large populations include blood pressure, shoe size, reading ability, and job satisfaction.

FIGURE 3-1

Example of a bell curve

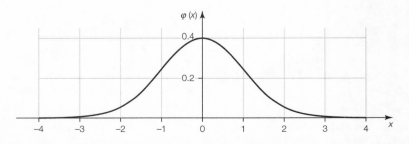

Source: *Normal distribution*, March 13, 2010 via Creative Commons Attribution 3.0. Courtesy of Geek3.

Iconic

It would be possible to imagine a market for music, art, books, or movies with a normal distribution. But that is not at all what cultural markets look like. They tend to look more like figure 3-2.

The most obvious feature of this graph is that a very small number of people are capturing a massive percentage of the returns. These are sometimes described as "winner-take-all" markets. Winners do not take *all*, of course; there is a long tail, and losers take something. Still, winners capture a remarkable percentage of the total. The graph below (figure 3-2) captures a power law distribution: it falls off a kind of cliff on the left and has a long tail to the right.

A power law is a relationship between two numbers in which a change in one produces a proportional change in the other, and in which the initial size of the two numbers does not matter.

FIGURE 3-2

A classic power law graph

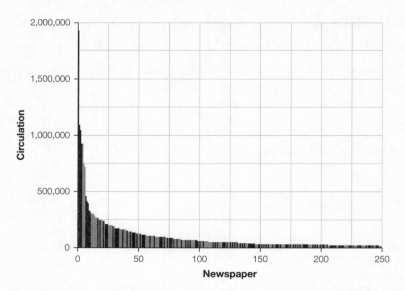

Source: Michael Tauberg, "Power Law in Popular Media," Medium, June 29, 2018, https://michaeltauberg
.medium.com/power-law-in-popular-media-7d7efef3fb7c.

Suppose, for example, that you double the length of the side of a square. The area of the square will be quadrupled. Or suppose that you double the length of the side of a cube. The area of the cube will be increased by a factor of eight. Under a power law, the probability of obtaining a certain value x is inversely proportional to x raised to the power of a constant a, known as the exponent. In the example of the square, the exponent is two; in the example of the cube, the exponent is 3.

None of this is intuitive. We are used to linear relationships. But a stunning number of patterns of success and failure show power law distributions. Figure 3-3, for example, shows a pattern for book sales, and figure 3-4 shows a pattern for songs.

FIGURE 3-3

Power law graph for books

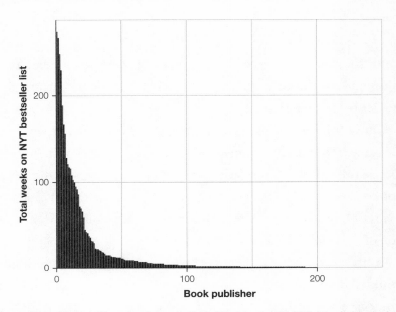

Source: Michael Tauberg, "Power Law in Popular Media," Medium, June 29, 2018, https://michaeltauberg .medium.com/power-law-in-popular-media-7d7efef3fb7c.

FIGURE 3-4

Power law graph for songs

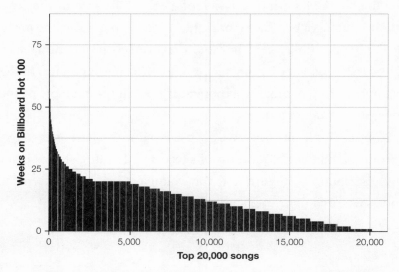

Top 20,000 songs

Source: Michael Tauberg, "Power Law in Popular Media," Medium, June 29, 2018, https://michaeltauberg.medium.com/power-law-in-popular-media-7d7efef3fb7c.

On the next page, figure 3-5 shows a pattern for video game sales, and on the following page figure 3-6 shows a pattern for movies by box office gross.

You will immediately have noticed that the graphs look about the same. It seems almost magical. The winners are spectacularly successful, and they are relatively few. In fact, power law distributions can be found in many domains, including the size of cities in terms of populations, the magnitude of earthquakes, the distribution of wealth, and executive compensation.

In literature, which poets get the most attention? You might think that there are a lot of extraordinary poets and that we would see something like a bell curve. But a careful study by

FIGURE 3-5

Power law graph for video games

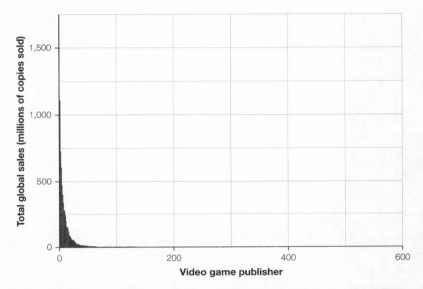

Source: Michael Tauberg, "Power Law in Popular Media," Medium, June 29, 2018, https://michaeltauberg .medium.com/power-law-in-popular-media-7d7efef3fb7c.

Colin Martindale finds that of 602 well-known poets listed in the *Oxford Book of English Verse*, a very small number are the subject of a very large number of books.[1] Martindale finds that 34,516 books were written about the 602 poets. Shakespeare accounted for 9,118, or 26.4 percent; 1,280 were about John Milton; 1,096 were about Chaucer. The top twelve authors accounted for about 50 percent of the books, and the top 25 authors accounted for 64.8 percent.

In fact, 22.3 percent of the poets are the subject of no books at all. Martindale makes a similar though less stark finding for the *Oxford Book of French Verse*: of 108 poets and 7,887 books,

FIGURE 3-6

Power law graph for movies

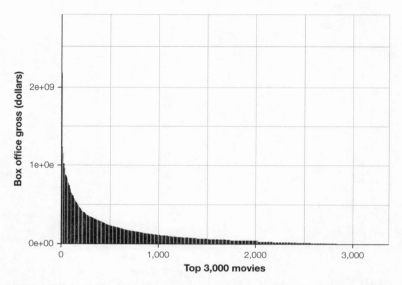

Source: Michael Tauberg, "Power Law in Popular Media," Medium, June 29, 2018, https://michaeltauberg .medium.com/power-law-in-popular-media-7d7efef3fb7c.

Voltaire is dominant, accounting for 10 percent, and more than half of the books focus on just ten of the authors. The conclusion is simple: "Literary fame is distributed in an extremely skewed fashion."[2] Martindale urges that the "more famous one is, the easier it is to become even more famous."[3]

One implication is that even if quality is skewed, it would be surprising to find that it is nearly as skewed as fame. Another implication is that fame gets "locked in," for "the leaders are so far ahead that it is hard to see how neglected authors could catch up."[4] As a result, our understanding of literary history— of who did what, and of who influenced whom—is bound to be distorted.

The Rich Get Richer

To get some clarity about why power law distributions occur, consider the Matthew Effect, identified and explored by the sociologist Robert Merton in 1968.[5] Merton named the Matthew Effect for a verse in the Gospel of Matthew, specifically Matthew 25:29, which reads, "For whosoever hath, to him shall be given, and he shall have more abundance: but whosoever hath not, from him shall be taken away even that he hath." In short, the rich get richer, and the poor get poorer. The intuitive idea is one of *cumulative advantage*, by which an initial advantage, or an acquired advantage, grows over time. That certainly happened to the *Mona Lisa* and the Beatles; it also happened to William Shakespeare, Leonardo da Vinci, Michelangelo, John Locke, Immanuel Kant, Virginia Woolf, Katherine Hepburn, Richard Wright, Tom Hanks, Stephen King, Harlan Coben, Daniel Kahneman, and Taylor Swift.

According to the Matthew Effect, the probability that someone or something will enjoy an increase in attention or popularity is directly proportional to the current attention it receives, or its current popularity. Once Stephen King becomes known as a terrific author, and as someone whom large numbers of people love, his appeal grows exponentially. As David Easley and Jon Kleinberg explain, "the more well known someone is, the more likely you are to hear their name come up in conversation, and hence the more likely you are to end up knowing about them as well."[6] That does not mean that a complete unknown cannot vault to the top. At one time, Stephen King was just a struggling writer. But it does mean that if you are doing really well, you are in an excellent position to do better still.

Merton found that once a scientist acquires a terrific reputation, things start to snowball. He focused on Nobel Prize laureates in particular and found that in cases of collaboration or independent discovery, it was the laureate who got the lion's share of the credit. He describes the Matthew Effect as consisting "in the accruing of greater increments of recognition for particular scientific contributions to scientists of considerable repute and the withholding of such recognition from scientists who have not yet made their mark."[7] With some gentleness, Merton added, "Laureates and other eminent men of science are sufficiently aware of this aspect of the Matthew effect to make special efforts to counteract it."[8] In their view, the effect creates "a basic inequity."

Merton seemed to agree with that assessment, and he urged that the phenomenon, and the inequity, extend well beyond Nobel Prize winners and the domain of science. In any case, "a scientific contribution will have greater visibility in the community of scientists when it is introduced by a scientist of high rank than when it is introduced by one who has not yet made his mark."[9] Merton links the effect with "the principle of cumulative advantage that operates in many systems of social stratification to produce the same result: the rich get richer at a rate that makes the poor become relatively poorer. Thus, centers of demonstrated scientific excellence are allocated far larger resources for investigation than centers which have yet to make their mark."[10] That is a point about science, but it extends far more generally to business, politics, culture and even sports.

A less-than-obvious implication of the principle of cumulative advantage is that success and failure can be exceedingly difficult to predict. How does one get a little bit rich, or a little bit popular, in the first place? Easley and Kleinberg imagine a world in which the Harry Potter books languish in obscurity: "If history were to be replayed multiple times, it seems likely that there would be a power-law distribution of popularity each of those times, but it's far from clear that the most popular items would always be the same."[11]

Informational Cascades

How come?

For a clue, note that what the Music Lab experiment uncovered was a set of *informational cascades*, a phenomenon that helps illuminate success and failure in multiple domains. The starting point is that people rationally attend to the informational signals given by the statements and action of others; we amplify the volume of the very signals by which we have been influenced. Consider Nazism and Communism; Elvis Presley, Eminem, Taylor Swift, and the Kardashians; Facebook and YouTube; Jane Austen and the *Mona Lisa*; the American Revolution, the movement for women's suffrage, the Arab Spring, Brexit, and the fall of Communism; #MeToo and Black Lives Matter; Critical Race Theory and the attack on wokeness. Cascade effects played a role in each of these cases.

Such effects can be found in all kinds of places. Connie Converse failed to benefit from cascade effects in her time; her music benefited from those effects long after her death. Was the rise of Christianity itself a product of an informational cascade? A careful historical account so suggests.[12] To be sure, we would like to go behind cascades themselves and to understand the specific factors that make them possible. But let us begin with the simple dynamics.

Imagine that seven people are in a reading group, deciding which book to try next. Assume that group members are announcing their views in sequence. Each person attends, reasonably enough, to the judgments of others. John is the first to speak. He suggests that a new book about the Beatles is the one to try. Paul, the second to speak, now knows John's judgment; he should certainly go along with John's recommendation if he is also enthusiastic about that book. But suppose that he does not really know; he is indifferent. If Paul trusts John, he might simply agree that the group should choose that new book.

Now turn to a third person, George. Suppose after both John and Paul have said that they want to try the book about the Beatles, George's own view, based on his own limited information, is that the book is not likely to be good. Even if George has that view, he might well ignore what he knows and just follow John and Paul. The reason is not that George is humble or cowardly. It is likely, after all, that both John and Paul have reasons for their enthusiasm. Unless George thinks that his own information is genuinely better than theirs, he ought to follow their lead. If he does, George is in a cascade. True, George will resist if he has sufficient grounds to think that John and Paul are being foolish. But if he lacks those grounds, he is likely to go along with them.

Now suppose that Ringo, Brian, Yoko, and Linda are expected to express their views. If John, Paul, and George have all said that the new book on the Beatles is the one to read, each of them might well reach the same conclusion (in sequence) even if they have some independent reason to think another choice would be better. In this example, the most important point is that the initial judgment by only one person (John) initiated a process by which people are led to participate in a cascade, leading the entire group to opt for a particular book. If John had suggested otherwise, or if Ringo had spoken first, the group might have made a radically different choice. It might have chosen something else, and perhaps helped to turn it into a big success.

This is, of course, a highly artificial and stylized example. But the basic process should be familiar, and it helps explain what happened in the Music Lab experiment and for countless now-iconic figures (including Batman, Barbie, and Wonder Woman), and also countless icons-that-never-were. People learn from others, and if some people seem to like something or to want to do something, others might like or do the same. This is so unless they have some reason to distrust them and if they lack a good reason to think that they are wrong. And in fact, informational cascades help explain a great deal about success and failure, and about fame and anonymity. As David Easley and Jon Kleinberg put it: "Fashions and fads, voting for popular candidates, the self-reinforcing success of books placed highly on bestseller lists, the spread of a technological choice by consumers and by firms, and the localized nature of crime and political movements can all be seen as examples of herding, in which people make decisions based on inferences from what earlier people have done."[13]

It is important to emphasize that economic models of informational cascades generally assume rational behavior. If you do not know whether a book, a movie, a laptop, or a song is good, it might well be reasonable for you to rely on the views of others, at least if you trust them (or do not distrust them). As the number of people who share the same view increases, relying on them becomes more reasonable still. The idea of the "wisdom of crowds" lies in this insight.

Nonetheless, there are problems. In the real world, *people tend to neglect the possibility that most of the people in the crowd might be in a cascade too and are not making independent judgments of their own.* Ringo might think that John, Paul, and George have all decided that a particular book is the one to read, when in fact John is the only person who has made that judgment. When observers see a dozen, a hundred, ten thousand, or two million people doing something, they might well underestimate the extent to which people are simply following their predecessors, and so overestimate the amount of information that is signaled by widespread popularity. A lot of people might be listening to a song, reading a book, or buying a product, but relatively few of them might be making independent judgments about what they should be listening to, reading, or buying. It is important to see that while informational cascades might produce large-scale changes in belief and behavior, those who participate in those cascades might be hearing a louder signal than they should.

It is also important to see that informational cascades might not be robust. They might produce fads or bubbles—and bubbles burst. As we have seen, Samuel Johnson was fully aware of the point. Suppose that John was wrong to select the new book about the Beatles and that the book is truly terrible. If so, he will learn that he was wrong and that the book is terrible, and so will the rest of the group's members. An informational cascade might lead people to download songs, to start to read a book, or to go to a movie theater, but can it actually lead people to *like* songs, finish books, or enjoy movies? The best answer, and the right one, is no.

Still, that answer is too simple. It is true that if people can tell that a song is terrible or dull, they will not enjoy it, even if they think that others have, and eventually, the song's popularity will wane. In this sense, informational cascades can be fragile. But for songs, movies, or other cultural products that rise above a certain threshold of quality, we cannot rule out the possibility that the reality or perception of widespread enthusiasm will lead to enduring success. People might develop a taste for something simply because others have led them to give it a try, and even if they do not exactly love it, they might say that they like it, or perhaps actually like it, because of the positive signals given by others.

Consider in this regard a different experiment from Salganik and his collaborator Duncan Watts.[14] That experiment drew on the Music Lab experiment, but with one exception: the experimenters *inverted the actual download figures*, so that participants would think that the least popular songs were the most popular, and the most popular songs the least. If quality is the real driver, one might expect that the worst songs (as measured by the independent judgment group) would eventually plummet to the bottom, and that the best ones (also as so measured) would eventually rise to the top.

Not at all! With the inversion, Salganik and Watts transformed the worst songs into significant successes and also made almost all of the top songs into colossal failures. Here, as in their principal experiment, the lesson is that people pay a great deal of attention to what other people appear to like, and that information about popularity can make all the difference. When publishers and authors work hard to promote early sales and "preorders," they know what they are doing. An especially high volume of early sales can vault a book to the bestseller list. And once a book gets on that list, there is a good chance that it will continue to do well.

In the inversion experiment, the wrinkle is that the very best song (again, as measured by actual popularity in the independent judgment tradition) always ended up doing quite well; social influences could not keep it down (though they could prevent it from being ranked at the very top).[15] With that wrinkle in mind, you might think that in the end, quality will produce success—or at least that exceptional quality will produce exceptional success. But as we have seen, that would be an unduly optimistic conclusion. The inversion experiment was also tightly controlled. In the real world, multiple factors can interfere with a march toward the top. Recall the tale of the *Mona Lisa*; we will see many other examples.

At Any Time

It is also important to note that informational cascades *can occur at any time*. A useful product—say, the iPhone or the MacBook—might benefit from a cascade from the inception, because it is useful. If it can be consistently improved, it might be a star performer for a long time. It might benefit from some kind of "lock-in." People know how to use the iPhone, and other cell phones, however wonderful and amazing, might be different, and learning how to use and enjoy what is different might seem daunting. Something similar can happen for music and books. As we have seen, people's tastes might be formed by what they know. Having developed a taste for the great Joyce Carol Oates, they might want to read more of what she has to offer. (Fortunately, she has a lot.)

Now, suppose that a poet, an artist, or a novelist did not do particularly well when young. It remains possible that they will be rediscovered, decades after they did their work, and become celebrated, with the aid of an informational cascade. Eve Babitz is just one example. (If you do not know her, look her up. Be prepared for some surprises.) As we have seen, it is entirely possible that fame will occur posthumously. Robert Johnson and Connie Converse are examples, and there are of course countless others. To compress a long story: Emily Dickinson died in 1886. Her friends and family knew that she was a poet, but almost no one else did. She published very little—a total of ten poems. She did write more than eighteen hundred poems. What should be done with them? Dickinson left no instructions.

Her sister, Lavinia Dickinson, insisted that they should be published. She wrote a friend: "I have had a 'Joan of Arc' feeling about Emilies [*sic*] poems from the first." Lavinia enlisted some of

Emily's friends to help. One of those friends was Mabel Loomis Todd, who was married to a professor at Amherst—and having an affair with Austin Dickinson, who was Emily's brother. Todd turned out to be crucial to Emily Dickinson's fame. Along with Thomas Wentworth Higginson, Dickinson's mentor, she coedited the first volume of Dickinson's work, *The Poems of Emily Dickinson*, which was published in 1890. They followed it with a second volume a year later. Some members of the public were immensely curious about this unknown poet. Higginson and Todd gave a number of lectures about her. That is what started everything.

Johann Sebastian Bach, who died in 1750, was widely known as a talented organ player and organ repair adviser. During his lifetime, Bach was also known as an outstanding performer, but not so much as a composer. Bach composed over a thousand works during his lifetime, but very few of them were published. He received a substantial boost in 1829, when composer Felix Mendelssohn popularized Bach's now-iconic piece, *The Passion of St. Matthew.*

Both Dickinson and Bach benefited from champions. That is a typical pattern with posthumous fame. Consider this title: *Jo van Gogh-Bonger: The Woman Who Made Vincent Famous.*[16] Van Gogh's extraordinary rise had a great deal to do with the relentless efforts of Jo van Gogh-Bonger, his sister-in-law, who devoted her life to promoting his work.

We will see other examples in chapter 5.

Reputational Cascades

With cultural products, ideas, politicians, and commercial goods, people may pay attention to the views of others because they want to know what is good. But sometimes what they most want is for other people to like them, or at least not to dislike them. They follow the views and actions of others for that reason. If most people are enthusiastic about a new song, a new book, or a new movie, they might show enthusiasm as well, or at least listen or look. We might do what others do because they are giving us a signal about what is good or right or true, but we might also follow them because we care what they think about us. The point might seem straightforward, but because it helps explain winner-take-all markets and some of the vagaries of fame, the underlying dynamics deserve attention.

In a reputational cascade, people think that they know what is right, or what is likely to be right, but they nonetheless go along with the crowd in order to maintain the good opinion of others. Suppose that Mick suggests that the Dave Clark Five is spectacular and that Keith concurs with Mick, not because he actually thinks that Mick is right, but because he does not wish to seem to Mick to be some kind of fool or idiot. If Mick and Keith say that the Dave Clark Five is terrific, Brian might not contradict them publicly and might even appear to share their judgment. This is not because he believes that judgment to be correct, but because he does not want to face their hostility or lose their good opinion.

It should be easy to see how this process might generate a cascade on behalf of the Dave Clark Five. Once Mick, Keith, and Brian offer a united front on the issue, their friend Charlie might be reluctant to contradict them even if he thinks that they are wrong. The apparently shared view of Mick, Keith, and Brian carries information; that view might be right. But even if Charlie has reason to believe that they are wrong, he might not want to take them on publicly. His own silence will help build the reputational pressure on those who follow.

In the Music Lab experiments, visitors to the site were not likely to be concerned about how their downloads affected their reputations. They were not necessarily friends or even acquaintances with one another. But when groups of people embrace a product, it is often because of the social pressure that comes from the apparent views of others.

Reputational cascades can also occur at any time. Robert Johnson, Emily Dickinson, and Bach certainly benefited from them.

Network Effects

Some things can be enjoyed by oneself. You might like a walk in the sun, a cup of coffee, or a quick swim, even or perhaps especially if you are alone. Other pleasures are guilty. One might love a silly television show or Tommy Roe (look him up), and one might not want to watch the show or listen to Tommy Roe with anyone else. But sometimes the value of a good depends on how many other people are using or enjoying it. It is not worthwhile to have a cell phone if you are the only person in the world who has a cell phone. People use Facebook because many people use Facebook. If Facebook had not been able to build a network, it would have failed.

Network effects exist when value increases with the number of users. Many cultural products benefit greatly from network effects: they are taken as something of which people think they should be aware. Shakespeare is an obvious example; those who do not know about him are obviously missing out. The old television show *The Twilight Zone* long benefited from network effects; people wanted to be part of a network of people who enjoyed and knew about *The Twilight Zone*. In 2023, *Barbie* and *Oppenheimer* benefited from network effects; people wanted to see *Barbie* and *Oppenheimer* because everyone else seemed to be seeing *Barbie* and *Oppenheimer*. Every culture has a set of iconic figures—poets, war heroes, politicians, religious leaders—who enjoy their current status in large part because of network effects.

Quite apart from the intrinsic merits of a song, a movie, or a television show, it might be good to know about it, so that one can talk to others about it. It might not be a lot of fun to stare blankly when someone makes a knowing reference to *Hamlet* or *King Lear,* or to *Star Wars: A New Hope,* or to "Yesterday," "Hey Jude," or "Let It Be," or to Barbie and Ken. If people see that other people like the Romantic poets or the Beatles and focus on them, they might join them for one reason above all: they do not want to be left out. They want to be part of the relevant group.

When books and movies benefit from exploding popularity, it is often because of network effects. Taylor Swift is terrific, one of my all-time favorites, but she is a massive success in part because people want to be part of the ever-growing group of people who know about and like or love Taylor Swift.

National holidays help constitute network effects. Martin Luther King Jr. would be famous even without a national holiday in his name, but the national holiday helps both to constitute and to memorialize the man as he is now understood. As we shall see, Stan Lee, the most important creative force behind Marvel Comics (Spider-Man, the Hulk, Thor, and many more) helped to create network effects and massively benefited from them. As we shall also see, something similar can be said of the *Star Wars* phenomenon.

Group Polarization

What happens when members of a group talk to one another? Group polarization is among the most robust patterns found in deliberating bodies, and it has been found in many diverse tasks.

In short, deliberating groups often end up pushing their members to extremes, including extreme enthusiasm, whether the issue involves a new product, a new idea, a possible leader, or a religious conviction.

Cults of various kinds often develop in this way. For products and persons, the implication is clear: If you want to create popularity or fame, take advantage of group polarization. Bob Dylan did that, and so did the Beatles, and so did Steve Jobs; in the 1950s and 1960s, Connie Converse did not.

Like-minded people, engaged in discussions with one another, can lead one another to manias of various sorts. In business and politics, that happens all the time. Tulipmania, in the Netherlands in the 1630s, is the most celebrated economic example; Beatlemania is another illustration. Group polarization usually arises spontaneously: People in a neighborhood, or in some online group, talk to one another about some person or product, and they fuel each other's excitement. But group polarization can be self-consciously induced.

Those who seek to spur enthusiasm for artists, singers, movies, politicians, and causes try to ensure that like-minded people are engaging with one another, increasing their excitement. Clubs of various kinds often do exactly that. As we shall see, Stan Lee and Marvel Comics were greatly helped by group polarization. In 1964, they created the Merry Marvel Marching Society, complete with membership cards and certificates. As we shall also see, Ayn Rand benefited from a process of that sort with the rise of her (stupid) philosophy of "objectivism," which helped to sell millions of books. She created something like "objectivism clubs."

The relevant work has been undertaken for more than fifty years. Consider some examples of the phenomenon of group polarization, which has been found in over a dozen nations.

- After discussion, Americans who are concerned about climate change, and who favor an international treaty to control it, become more firmly committed to those beliefs.[17]

- After discussion, Americans who are not especially concerned about climate change, and do not favor an international treaty to control it, become even less enthusiastic about such a treaty.[18]

- After discussion, citizens of France become more critical of the United States and its intentions with respect to economic aid.[19]

- A group of moderately pro-feminist women becomes more strongly pro-feminist after discussion with one another.[20]

- After discussion, whites predisposed to show racial prejudice offer more negative responses to the question whether white racism is responsible for conditions faced by African Americans in American cities.[21]

- After discussion, whites predisposed not to show racial prejudice offer more positive responses to the same question.[22]

These are mostly political issues, and if you are interested in how political divisions arise, group polarization is a good place to start. It is also a good place to begin if the goal is to understand why businesses make terrible decisions. But my topic here is fame, and group polarization offers strong clues. As statistical regularities, those moderately enthusiastic about a politician, a poem, a movie, a song, or a novel will, after discussion, grow in their enthusiasm. Consider Beatlemania in this light, and note that concerts are often case studies in group polarization.

Of course, it is also true that some people may remain outliers, either because they really do not like the direction in which the group is going (and are willing to say so), or because they are rebels by nature. After all, some people do not like the Beatles, and many people resist cultural enthusiasms. But by definition, they are outliers, and they may even be misfits.

There are three main explanations for why group polarization occurs. All of them help account for the success of politicians, poets, movies, songs, novels, actors, and products. They certainly help to explain fame.

The first explanation emphasizes the simple role of information exchange. It starts with a simple claim: any individual's position on any topic is partly a function of what information is presented, and of which points, supposed facts, or arguments presented within the group seem convincing. People's judgments move in the direction of the most persuasive position defended by the group, taken as a whole.

If most people in a group think that Connie Converse is terrific, and defend that view with energy and conviction, other people will probably be influenced. If most people in a group think that Shakespeare is overrated, and that Samuel Beckett wrote better plays, other group members might well think: maybe so! Here is the key point: because a group whose members are already inclined in a certain direction will likely hear a large number of arguments supporting that same direction, the result of discussion will be to move people further in the direction of their initial inclinations.

The second points to the relationship among corroboration, confidence, and extremism. People who lack confidence, and who are unsure what they should think, tend to moderate their views. It is for this reason that cautious people, not knowing what to say or do, are likely to choose the midpoint between relevant extremes.

You might not express a great deal of enthusiasm for the work of Joyce Carol Oates when you do not know what people around you think. But if other people seem to share your view, and keep saying (rightly) that Oates is terrific, you are likely to become more confident that that view is right—and hence to move in a more extreme direction.

Enthusiasm for musicians, artists, and writers often intensifies in this way. The Beatles are a case in point, and so are the Doors, to point to just one other example in the domain of classic rock music. Their fans participated in a process of group polarization. Barack Obama and Donald Trump benefited from a similar process. So have prominent figures in the history of religion. So have certain products, including the iPhone, Tesla, and Earl Grey tea.

The final explanation begins with the claim that people care about their reputations. They want to be perceived favorably by other group members. They also want to perceive themselves favorably. Once people hear what others believe, they adjust their positions in the direction of the dominant position. They may want to signal, for example, that they are not cowardly or cautious. Thus individuals move their judgments in order to preserve their image to others and their image to themselves. Is Beatlemania an illustration? Is the iconic status of the *Mona Lisa*? No doubt about it.

Oprah's Book Club

Can these various effects be combined? Is there a way to make that likely to happen?

For a vivid illustration, consider Oprah Winfrey's Book Club, which initially ran from September 1996 to April 2002. In that period, Winfrey was extraordinarily famous, with a TV talk show that was watched by millions of viewers. She was also trusted and admired. During the relevant period, she made forty-eight book recommendations.

Here is the question: What was the impact of being selected by Oprah? You might speculate that it would be pretty large in the short run, but not in the long run. Or you might think that she could give a book a little boost for a day or two, or maybe even a week, but not for much longer than that. Even Oprah Winfrey could not work miracles. Perhaps quality would ultimately prevail, and books would return to the place they would otherwise be, no matter what Winfrey recommended. (If you are thinking that this is a bit like a real-world version of the Music Lab experiment, with selection by Oprah being the equivalent of a large number of early downloads—well, I think so too.)

Richard Butler, Benjamin Cowan, and Sebastian Nilsson have investigated the impact of being selected by Oprah.[23] Their conclusion is signaled by their title: "From Obscurity to Bestseller." The central finding is that *not one* of the forty-eight books was in the top 150 bestsellers in the United States in the week before Winfrey recommended them, but that *every one* of them made the list in the week after. Winfrey's picks made that list not for a very short period, but for at least three months. More dramatically, the strong majority of Oprah's selections had *never* been on that list before, and the highest ranking that any of them had achieved was 25. Still, every one of Oprah's first eleven selections made it at least into the top *four*.

You might speculate that those selections would surely do less well than the average bestseller. If so, your speculation would be reasonable—but wrong. Her selections stayed on the bestseller list at least as long as and perhaps a bit longer than other bestsellers. Indeed, several of her selections had multiple runs as bestsellers, and fourteen of them ended up in the top 150 as *paperbacks*. It is worth underlining that finding. On average, the fourteen paperbacks became bestsellers forty-two weeks after Oprah picked them.

The basic point is that if Winfrey endorsed a book, it was guaranteed to become a bestseller, and then to enjoy strong sales for months. For retail bookstores, an Oprah pick produced about $80 million in new sales.

Why did that happen? It makes sense to think of an endorsement by Oprah as equivalent to a lot of early downloads, amplified by four important facts:

1. She had a great deal of credibility in her audience, which trusted what she had to say.

2. Because her endorsement was known to drive sales, it produced an immediate network effect.

3. Booksellers themselves knew what was coming, and put her picks on display.

4. People thought that it would be a good idea to read one of her picks, so as not to be left out.

Oprah Winfrey was (and is) unique, of course, but these are not meant only (or mostly) as points about how her picks fared. As we will see, pre-Oprah Oprahs, of various sorts, are responsible for the fame of some of the greatest literary figures in the English language. As we will also see, pre-Oprah Oprahs, many of them lost to the history books, account for the rise of many of our icons. Of course, there are post-Oprah Ophrahs as well; with respect to Connie Converse, Howard Fishman is one.

Better Off Dead

Here is a question: Do you think that writers, artists, and musicians will sell more of their work in the period immediately after they die? Is death good for business?

A possible answer is: definitely not. People either do or do not like the Beatles, Frank Sinatra, Picasso, John Updike, and Janis Joplin, and whether they buy books, paintings, or music will depend on whether they expect to like the work, not on whether the person responsible for them is living and in good health. Whether a writer has died should be a matter of indifference—just as it is a matter of indifference whether a writer is married or single, or young or old, rich or poor. The work is what matters.

As it turns out, this reasonable answer appears to be wrong. We don't know exactly why, but death does appear to be good for business. As Gore Vidal said when told of the death of Truman Capote, "a wise career move."[24] Vidal was onto something.

The most careful work comes from Italy, where the economists Michela Ponzo and Vincenzo Scoppa studied the effects of a writer's death on book sales.[25] The central finding is that in the period after an author dies, the probability that he or she will be on the bestseller list leaps dramatically. Indeed, it increases by more than 100 percent!

Ponzo and Scoppa also find if you want to make the bestseller list, you are a lot better off dying young. Writers who died at or under the age of 65 enjoy a significantly bigger "death bonus" than do writers who died over that age. In addition, media attention makes a big difference. For book sales, the beneficial effect of death is concentrated in writers whose death is on the front page and is otherwise covered prominently and often. Broadly similar findings have been made for artists: the price of their paintings increases after death, and the effect has been found to be larger for artists who die young.[26]

These findings raise many questions. Let's fuss a bit. If you took the full universe of writers in the world, and ask whether their sales jumped after their death, the answer is overwhelmingly likely to be a firm no. There are approximately a zillion writers in the world right now, and the number of people who actually publish a book in any given year is probably in the vicinity of four million. (That is the annual number of books, and while some authors publish more than one per year—I plead guilty as charged—four million annual authors is unlikely to be far off.[27]) If we estimate that about nine of one thousand people die every year, we might estimate that very roughly, thirty-six thousand of those four million published authors will die annually.[28]

How many of them enjoy a big boost in sales? Undoubtedly very few! Most writers don't sell many books at any time, and the year after their death isn't any better than the year before their death. If you are an obscure writer (and most writers are obscure), you should not think that if you die, your books are going to take off.

Ponzo and Scoppa limited their research to writers who had at least one book on the bestseller list, and they used a set of ingenious strategies to test whether writers become more likely to end up on the list six months after their death. All this means that we have to say that *if we focus only on writers with a certain level of renown, sales might well increase after death, at least if their death receives serious newspaper attention.*

That's an important finding. What's behind it? The simplest explanation points to attention. When well-known authors die, people focus on them. You might not think about Joyce Carol Oates or Mick Jagger very much, but if either dies (and here's a hope that neither ever does), a lot of people will suddenly think about them a fair bit—and go right out and buy their work. In a way, death is like a well-financed publicity campaign, or like being chosen by Oprah Winfrey, and it can work for the same reason. Death can also create an instant network effect: people might think that other people are going to be reading or listening to the deceased, and that they ought to join them.

Emotions undoubtedly matter as well. Many of us feel connected to well-known writers, and death produces a period of grief and mourning. One way to handle those feelings is to spend time with the deceased, and in that way to stay connected with them. If you lose someone you love, you might cherish photographs and letters. Writers and artists might be people you love, or at least to whom you feel attached; they might be part of the fabric of your life. Their work is the equivalent of photographs and letters. You want to linger over them.

CHAPTER 4

The Elephant in the Room

There is an elephant in the room.

In 1991, I was teaching at the University of Chicago Law School. Michael McConnell, a colleague and friend of mine, was head of the Appointments Committee, which meant that he was in charge of hiring new faculty. He told me that he had worked with a student at Harvard Law School, who would, he thought, be a superb law professor. I asked McConnell for the student's name.

He said, "It's an unusual name." I said, "Oh?" He responded: "Yes. Barack Obama."

As you may know, Obama did end up teaching at the University of Chicago Law School. He was obviously a leader; there was something about the way he carried himself. In 1999 or so, I happened to run into him in front of the Seminary Co-op Bookstore in Chicago, and I blurted out what seemed obvious: "You will be president of the United States one day." But when he ran for the United States Senate in 2003, his friends and colleagues in Chicago thought that while he would be a terrific politician, he had two serious challenges: he was Black, and his name was Barack Obama. As everyone now knows, he overcame those challenges. He was elected to the Senate in 2004, and then as president in 2008.

Yes, he had a ton of luck, and yes, he benefited from a lot of early downloads, and yes, he enjoyed something a lot like Beatlemania, and yes, informational cascades, reputational cascades, network effects, and group polarization were key to his success—but that is a story for another day. What I want to emphasize is that although Obama was extraordinary on the campaign trail, it is reasonable to doubt whether he could have been elected in 1948, or 1960, or 1968, or 1972, or 1980, or even 1984. A Black candidate named Barack Obama would probably have faced too much opposition in those years.

In 2008, the fact that Obama was Black turned out not be a decisive barrier; for many voters, it was a positive. Many people thought: *Isn't it about time that the United States of America had a Black president? Wouldn't a Black president say something, to the United States and the world, about what freedom really means?*

This is not only a point about Barack Obama. In countless domains, including business, politics, music, art, film, and literature, success or failure, and fame, are affected by factors of this sort—by what we might think of as politics, writ large.

Real opportunity does not come to many. Wealth, religion, gender, and race are obviously relevant. Seeking to succeed in some domain in 1740, a woman might face insurmountable barriers. She might do extraordinary work, but she might be disparaged or ignored, and she might give up. Or she might not try at all. Jane Franklin, obscure sister of Benjamin Franklin, and perhaps as talented as he (who knows?), became obsessed by the arguments of Richard Price, who was much focused on the importance of starting points, which doom so many.[1]

"Dr. Price," Jane wrote to Benjamin, "thinks Thousands of Boyles Clarks and Newtons have Probably been lost to the world, and lived and died in Ignorance and meanness, merely for want of being Placed in favourable Situations, and Injoying Proper Advantages."[2] Jane's lament was personal. As Jill Lepore writes, "Benjamin Franklin thought of his sister as his 'Second Self,' and of the family's seventeen (!) children, no two were more alike."[3] And while Benjamin became an icon, one of the leading literary and scientific thinkers in the entire history of the American Republic, Jane's education was stunted, despite her keen interest in reading and writing.

This problem is the theme of Virginia Woolf's *A Room of One's Own*. Consider this passage, discussing Shakespeare's imaginary sister, as talented as he:

[It] would have been impossible, completely and entirely, for any woman to have written the plays of Shakespeare in the age of Shakespeare. Let me imagine, since facts are so hard to come by, what would have happened had Shakespeare had a wonderfully gifted sister, called Judith, let us say. . . . She was as adventurous, as imaginative, as agog to see the world as he was. But she was not sent to school. She had no chance of learning grammar and logic, let alone of reading Horace and Virgil. . . . Perhaps she scribbled some pages up in an apple loft on the sly, but was careful to hide them or set fire to them. Soon, however, before she was out of her teens, she was to be betrothed to the son of a neighboring wool stapler. She cried out that marriage was hateful to her, and for that she was severely beaten by her father. Then he ceased to scold her. He begged her instead not to hurt him, not to shame him in this matter of her marriage. He would give her a chain of beads or a fine petticoat, he said; and there were tears in his eyes. How could she disobey him? How could she break his heart?[4]

Centuries later, the same woman is likely to be much better off. And at some point, a woman who produced in her youth, but did not succeed, might be rediscovered and celebrated. For three of countless examples, look up Constance Fenimore Woolson, Bette Howland, or Eve Babitz.

Or consider the astoundingly prolific Margaret Cavendish, born in the United Kingdom in 1623, who was a philosopher, a playwright, a poet, and more. Cavendish much sought fame, but in her time, she did not get it. Indeed, she was not especially well regarded in the centuries since her death. Virginia Woolf claimed that Cavendish "frittered her time away scribbling nonsense and plunging ever deeper into obscurity and folly."

In recent years, she has become widely admired; her work is taught in colleges and universities, and philosophers grapple with her ideas. Cavendish was a materialist; she objected to mind-body dualism, of the sort embraced by Descartes, and she can easily be seen as an early feminist, critical of gender hierarchy. She was extraordinarily ambitious and wide-ranging; she even wrote science fiction. Before long, she might become some kind of philosophical canon.

If that happens, it might well be because she was genuinely great. But it might also be partly *because* she was a woman, or because current readers are more enthusiastic about what she had to say, or because they are prepared to respond to it as her contemporaries were not. In general, what was once a problem or an obstacle can disappear as such; it can even be turned into a benefit or a bonus. What was once a kind of tax-on-being-female can be repealed, or turned into a subsidy.

Marginalization

Jeanne Peijnenburg and Sander Verhaegh, Danish philosophers, have studied what they call "historiographical marginalization."[5] They focus on people, and particularly women, who were admired during their lifetime but whose work "never entered the canon because historians and textbook authors for some reason chose not to include it in their overviews." As they note, some people are marginalized even during their lifetime. They offer the example of Grete Hermann, a German mathematician, physicist, and philosopher who did not get the recognition she deserved, even though she uncovered a serious flaw in some foundational work by the mathematician John von Neumann. They note that "the history of 20th century physics would have been different if" Hermann's work had received the attention it was due.

But Peijnenburg and Verhaegh are especially concerned with people, and especially women, who disappear over time. They draw attention to the work of Constance Jones (1849–1922), who solved a famous puzzle in logic, and who was an admired and respected philosopher in her lifetime, but who was not featured in handbooks, textbooks, or anthologies. Jones is now having a revival. Peijnenburg and Verhaegh point as well to Suzanne Langer (1895–1985), an American who was a leader in the field of analytic philosophy. Langer's 1942 book, *Philosophy in a New Key*, was reprinted, and reprinted again, and reprinted again, and sold more than half a million copies. But over the years, she began to be ignored, perhaps because she emphasized the study of rituals, myths, and art. By the late 1940s, she had become widely ignored. In analytic philosophy, she is now widely forgotten.

Peijnenburg and Verhaegh draw attention to the role of historical and other factors in shaping the arc of philosophical thought. In the 1930s, for example, members of the Vienna Circle left Europe for the United States and England, where they had a massive impact on the rise of logical positivism. Peijnenburg and Verhaegh urge that philosophers tend wrongly to focus on a few key figures, and deprive us of a "a broader and intellectually more diverse canon." They do not think that we can "go back in time and undo the processes that pushed female philosophers into the periphery." But they do believe that it is important and possible to correct "the omissions, oversights, and even downright mistakes our predecessors made in writing about (or worse, not writing about) the contributions of female philosophers." And indeed, that kind of correction, often in the form of historical recovery, is very much taking place.[6]

Some people, including Cavendish, are said to have been "ahead of their time." What they thought, and what they did, was not appreciated by their contemporaries; people were "not ready for them." But it is not clear what these words mean. It might be that someone was not struck by lightning during their lives, but after their death, lightning struck; they started to get downloads, perhaps by accident. That is true, I think, of Vincent van Gogh and Herman Melville. Or it might be that their work just did not resonate, not because of bad luck, but because people at the time were not receptive to it.

Robert Johnson and Connie Converse might well be cases in point. It might be that a particular view of something—religion, race, politics, rebellion, gender, class, romance—seemed outlandish, eccentric, boring, or beyond the pale at one point. But it seems thrilling at another point.

A Great Hero

In any nation, and at any point, who is celebrated, who is vil-ified, and who is ignored? Who and what is remembered? Who are history's heroes? Some chilling words from George Orwell's *1984*: "Every record has been destroyed or falsified, every book has been rewritten, every picture has been repainted, every statue and street and building has been renamed, every date has been altered."[7] Outside of fictional accounts, we can ask about memory and about heroes over a span of generations—the intergenerational case. It can also be asked over a span of years or months or even weeks—the intragenerational case.

I was thirteen years old when Martin Luther King Jr. was assas-sinated. I remember him well. In my mother's view, he was a heroic and admirable figure (though she also said, at one point over dinner, that he was a "rabble-rouser"; I had no idea what those words meant). But who knew, at the time, what an icon King would become? Who knew that a national holiday would be named in his honor?

Yesterday's demon is today's saint. Yesterday's oracle is today's heretic. Yesterday's superstar is today's has-been. What happens across time can happen across space as well, both across nations and within them. (Remember "Remember the Alamo?") Debates about "collective memory" are often debates about exactly these points.[8]

Many years ago, I received a lesson to this general effect in Bei-jing. During a tour of a museum, my Chinese host brought me to an exhibit about Genghis Khan. I did not know much about him, but I did know one thing, which is that he was a satanic figure. I immediately recoiled and said, "A terrible tyrant." My host seemed shocked and replied, "No, a great hero." I felt embarrassed, as if I had made a faux pas, and I said with a sheepish smile: "American propaganda." He responded with a smile and what seemed like a secret acknowledgment: "Chinese propaganda."

In the United States, those associated with the Old South, including Robert E. Lee, have sometimes been lionized in collective memory, not least through statues that celebrate them. The many efforts to take down those statues, and to demote those who fought for the Old South, are examples of the kinds of contests that lead to the elevation and demotion of politicians, artists, and figures of many different sorts, both within their lifetime and thereafter.

Consider a vivid example from the sociologist Lewis Coser.[9] Coser noticed that in the 1980s, some of his Soviet colleagues (yes, the Soviet Union still existed) were hesitant even to discuss recent events. The reason was that they "had been forced in the last few years to shed their own collective memory like a skin, and to reconstruct a largely different set of collective memories." That is not easy, especially when "major historical figures who had been killed, slandered, vilified under Stalin were now shown to have been good Bolsheviks and major revolutionary heroes." History had been rewritten. This is an Orwellian tale, of course, with political leaders recasting the past: What's up is down; what's down is up. Thus Orwell:

> Every record has been destroyed or falsified, every book rewritten, every picture has been repainted, every statue and street building has been renamed, every date has been altered. And the process is continuing day by day and minute by minute. History has stopped. Nothing exists except an endless present in which the Party is always right.[10]

In Coser's telling, people who had been demonized were turned into heroes. That shift was particularly dramatic in the latest days of the Soviet Union, and of course it is vivid when it happens in nondemocratic societies. But it happens even in the freest of free societies, as new values and commitments cast, say, Malcolm X and Robert E. Lee in a radically different light. It can also happen when someone who was unknown becomes celebrated and lionized, and when someone who was a giant is belittled and disappeared (or canceled). Now ask about historical events and, say, about Nazism, World War II, and the Holocaust.[11] Do we remember? What do we remember in the 1960s? In the 1990s? Now? In Germany? In France? In Russia?

In the 1920s, Maurice Halbwachs, to whom we will turn shortly, offered an extraordinary discussion of the topography of Christianity—of how we know what happened where and when. His conclusion is that much of what we think we know, about the holy sites and much else, does not come from the time that Jesus lived. Much of it is speculation, or perhaps an invention. Here is what Halbwachs has to say:

> The apocryphal tales of the childhood of Jesus, of the youth, the life, and the death of Mary, the mystical meditations on the mystery of the cross, the mystery plays presented in the churches of the Middle Ages, the whole religious iconography of the cathedrals, these were what the pilgrims wished to find again, to situate, to put into place. This attests to the fact that in each period the collective Christian memory adapts its recollections of the details of Christ's life and of the places where they occurred to the contemporary exigencies of Christianity, its needs and aspirations.[12]

Pause over "the contemporary exigencies of Christianity, its needs and aspirations." The general point has to do with the Zeitgeist, or the prevailing spirit of the age, or the concerns and preoccupations of a powerful, important, or relevant audience.

James Baldwin, who died in 1987, was celebrated in his time as an exceedingly important writer, above all about race. For a time, he seemed to have been marginalized. As of this writing, he is enjoying a significant rebirth, in large part because his work speaks to contemporary issues. Or consider King himself. Was he a radical, or was he essentially a conservative? Did he call for large-scale social and economic changes, designed to eliminate white supremacy? Or was he a moderate, calling for a principle of colorblindness? Different people are appropriating King for different purposes and in light of contemporary exigencies, needs, and aspirations.

As we shall see, Stan Lee, the creator or cocreator of many of the world's most famous superheroes, succeeded in the 1960s in large part because his defiant, vulnerable characters spoke directly to the temper of the time. As we shall also see, William Blake and Jane Austen have enjoyed cultlike success long after their deaths, in part because they spoke to relevant groups at relevant times.

It is important to be careful with Zeitgeist-type arguments. They are easier to make than to prove. Still, they help explain why lightning strikes.

Remembering Together

The most luminous account of collective memory comes from Halbwachs, who gives considerable attention to religious memory.[13] What do people remember about the history of their own religion? Halbwachs emphasizes that "the memory of religious groups claims to be fixed once and for all."[14] This is a puzzle, because in its early stages, religions have diverse and competing strands, many of which consist of beliefs, rituals, and traditions of older religions. Early on, "Christianity was in effect very close to its origins; it wasn't yet easy to distinguish what was remembrance from what was consciousness of the present."[15]

In the early days, the same events are "remembered" very differently. "What distinguishes heresies from more or less orthodox doctrines is not that the first are inspired by the present or the recent past while the others draw on an ancient past; rather it is the way in which each recalls and understands the same period of the past which is still close enough for there to exist a great variety of remembrances and of witnesses."[16]

It is worth pausing over this point. At any moment, there may be competing memories of what happened the week before, or the month before. Consider this: What happened in the United States on January 6, 2021? Who were the heroes and who were the villains? Or consider this: What were the roles of the United States, England, and the Soviet Union in World War II?

In the formative period, collective memory is, in Halbwachs's account, highly dispersed. Nothing is frozen or congealed. After a long time, some understandings have risen and become fixed; those understandings include the heroes and the heretics, the sinners and the saints, the winners and the losers. Still (and this is one of Halbwachs's most striking claims): "A Catholic living ten or fifteen centuries later will understand the Gospels less well than a pagan, a Jew, an Oriental, or a Roman of the first two centuries."[17]

In Halbwachs's account, the first generation was crucial in part because it was highly creative. It invented something. For Christianity, that generation established the essentials of the

Christian tradition "through alterations and by a labor of adaptation."[18] In that period, "the image of Christ as Jewish prophet and Galilean was replaced by that of Christ as savior of all mankind," which meant that "the properly Jewish traits of Jesus—which must have been familiar to those around him—had either to fall into oblivion or be transposed."[19] It is a little bit like the Music Lab.

Could things have been otherwise? "When thinking about memory," writes Aleida Assmann, "we must start with forgetting."[20]

As memories fade, and as religions rise and shift, contemporary values and needs matter. Return to Martin Luther King Jr.; Was he essentially a centrist, calling for racial neutrality, or was he a radical, calling for an end to a system of racial caste? Halbwachs points to the central role of Christian mystics, who sought to revive "poorly known or neglected aspects of the sacred writings," not in an objective inquiry into history, but "because these aspects respond to the more or less conscious religious aspirations that existed within the mystics even before they focused their thoughts on those texts."[21] More broadly, the tradition of the Church includes "an entire series of particular traditions, which seem to disappear in certain periods but to reappear in others."[22]

To say the least, the rise and reformation of religions is a complicated and fraught topic. For present purposes, a central point is that the identity of the central figures—who is celebrated or remembered and who is lost or forgotten—is an act of construction, and it might turn out to depend on relative accidents, and who says or does what, and exactly when. The much-debated question of how books became part of the Bible, and hence defining of Christianity, illustrates the point.[23] Halbwachs himself does not much explore a possible implication of his analysis, which is that with respect to religion, things could have turned out quite differently. But he does say this:

> Let us suppose that Christianity was never propagated beyond its place of origin. In this case the Christian sect would have remained what it started out to be: a very small part of the old Jewish society. The latter would have tried to smother or eliminate it. The story of Christ would have been forgotten rather quickly—to the degree that the material traces of the Christian facts disappeared.[24]

Might we imagine a counterfactual world in which Christianity did indeed disappear, or had a significantly different form? It is very difficult, of course, to answer such questions with confidence. Science fiction writers, rather than historians, tend to paint vivid pictures. Can you imagine a world in which Gnosticism triumphed? What would such a world be like?[25] It is surely possible to imagine a New Testament that is different from the one we know, and that significantly altered what Christianity is now taken to be. This is hardly the place for a detailed treatment, but note that Matthew, Mark, Luke, and John—the canonical Gospels—are generally believed to have been written between AD 70 and AD 100, with the modern names being added well after, probably between the second and fourth centuries.

The current canon was the product of a series of fierce disputes and contested choices, and it was likely a response, in part, to those who strongly favored different choices.[26] Other books, not part of the New Testament as we understand it, were called "Scripture" well into the fourth and fifth centuries, and possibly later still.[27] Informational cascades, reputational cascades, network effects, and group polarization were crucial to the establishment of the canon. "Jesus himself never wrote a book and neither did he tell any of his followers to write a book," and much of the original transmission was oral.[28] And notably, the books of the New Testament "were not written as *sacred Scripture*."[29]

Here's a summary from an authoritative treatment; please note the centuries as they pass:

> From the first third of the second century, some early Christian texts began to be recognized as sacred scripture on par with the church's first Scriptures. By the last quarter of the second century a collection of Christian writings had begun to be called "New Testament" scriptures and the church's first two Testaments formed what later eventually was called the Christian Bible. By the third or fourth centuries, some followers of Jesus began to limit their sacred Scripture to a collection that roughly parallels what comprises the Christian Bibles today.[30]

As Elaine Pagels urges, "It is the winners who write history—their way. No wonder, then, that the viewpoint of the successful majority has dominated all traditional accounts of the origin of Christianity."[31] Indeed, the "New Testament Scriptures of the earliest Christian churches differ in a number of respects from those that most Christians use today," including "the books contained in them" and "the texts of those books."[32]

Canons

Of course, we might say something analogous about "canons" of all kinds—literary, philosophical, artistic, musical, cinematic, and otherwise—and about stability and change over time.[33] When philosophers invoke a tradition, who is included?[34] Kant and Bentham? Williams and Parfit? Who is in the canon of "rock music"?[35] The Jefferson Airplane? Jethro Tull? Suzanne Vega? Who appears in the standard literary anthologies? Who is omitted? Harold Bloom writes that Milton's *Paradise Lost* "became canonical before the secular Canon was established in the century after Milton's own."[36] And who did the canonizing? Bloom points to "other strong poets, from his friend Andrew Marvell through John Dryden and on to nearly every crucial poet of the eighteenth century and the Romantic period," to the point where Milton "simply overwhelmed the tradition and subsumed it."[37]

The great literary critic Hugh Kenner once puzzled over the following fact: "No Englishman alive in 1600 was living in the age of Shakespeare. For there was no age of Shakespeare in 1600."[38] Kenner went further. In 1600, there simply was no canon. And at the time, except for theater circles, Shakespeare was not "even so much as a celebrity." What happened?

It's a long story. John Heminges and Henry Condell were a crucial part of it. Have you heard of them? They were actors. They acted with Shakespeare, and they were his friends. After he died, they put his plays together in the famous First Folio of 1623. Without it, we would probably have only about half of Shakespeare's plays; we would have lost *Julius Caesar*, *The Tempest*, and *Macbeth*. For a flavor, here's what the editors wrote by way of preface:

It had bene a thing, we confesse, worthie to haue bene wished, that the Author himselfe had liu'd to haue set forth, and ouerseen his owne writings; But since it hath bin ordain'd otherwise, and he by death departed from that right, we pray you do not envie his Friends, the office of their care, and paine, to haue collected &publish'd them; and so to haue publish'd them, as where (before) you were abus'd with diuerse stolne, and surreptitious copies, maimed, and deformed by the frauds and stealthes of iniurious imposters, that expos'd them: euen those, are now offer'd to your view cur'd, and perfect of their limbes; and all the rest, absolute in their numbers, as he conceiued them. . . . But it is not our prouince, who onely gather his works, and giue them you, to praise him. It is yours that reade him.[39]

Wow.

When I was an undergraduate in the 1970s, majoring in English, the foundation for our curriculum was laid by *The Norton Anthology of English Literature*. Words cannot do justice to how much I loved and cherished the *Norton Anthology*. Offhand, and from memory: *Beowulf*, Chaucer, Milton (of course), John Donne, George Herbert, Keats, Byron, Tennyson, Matthew Arnold, T. S. Eliot. And the sublime, astonishing Gerard Manley Hopkins, with the devastating last line:

Márgarét, áre you gríeving
Over Goldengrove unleaving?
Leáves like the things of man, you
With your fresh thoughts care for, can you?
[. . .]
It ís the blight man was born for,
It is Margaret you mourn for.[40]

Harold Bloom writes that people break "into the canon only by aesthetic strength, which is constituted primarily of an amalgam: mastery of figurative language, originality, cognitive power, knowledge, exuberance of diction."[41] Back in the 1970s, I thought something roughly like that. I felt that the contents of the *Norton Anthology* were immutable and came from on high—not from a person, or from people, who actually made contestable choices. But the *Norton Anthology* was not the same in the 1990s as it was in the 1970s, and it is not the same now as it was in the 1990s.[42] (Is that shocking?)

In particular, more recent editions of the *Norton Anthology* have featured more diverse groups of authors in many parts of the book. In the *Norton Anthology*'s coverage of the Romantic period, the first two editions lacked any author section on a female author. Female authors were slowly added, first in the third edition (Dorothy Wordsworth), and then gradually over time.[43] In the fourth edition, the editors added a thematic section called "The Woman Question."[44] In the seventh edition, the editors added new thematic sections on "slavery, the French Revolution, and the end of the British Empire."[45] In the eighth edition, a "Women in Power" section was added.[46]

Cascade effects and group polarization matter here as well. They are central to canon formation in numerous fields, and here too, there are multiple equilibria. Bloom was selecting on the dependent variable. Some of today's canon could be in tomorrow's trash.[47] We will return to these points in chapter 5.

Quality

I have not said a great deal about quality, except to note the self-evident point that it is, in some sense, a necessary condition for success, even if it is not a sufficient condition for success. There are, of course, challenging questions here—about whether this is always true, about what "in some sense" means, and about what quality is and how to measure it. Terrible movies can get very famous. For example, *Avatar* is terrible. (But it does have terrific special effects.) Terrible books can sell a lot of copies. Consider, or don't consider, the execrable Left Behind series. (But it does have drama.)

Sometimes it is possible to measure quality objectively. We should be able to specify what makes for quality in a sprinter or a marathon runner, or for that matter a cell phone, a laptop, a refrigerator, or a motor vehicle. Surely we can say a great deal about quality in literature, art, and music. But for many things, what we say about quality, in advance or even at the time, will be less helpful than we might hope, if the goal is to foresee spectacular success or enduring appeal.

In his passionate book on the Western canon, Bloom has a great deal to say about quality, and on why authors and works turn out to be canonical.[48] He urges that the "answer, more often than not, has turned out to be strangeness, a mode of originality that either cannot be assimilated, or that so assimilates us that we cease to see it as strange." That is a striking formulation. It is a plausible description of (for example) William Blake, John Donne, Gerard Manley Hopkins, James Joyce, Emily Dickinson, Samuel Beckett, and Bob Dylan. But there is a lot of impossible-to-assimilate strangeness out there, and most of it does not become canonical. Charles Dickens, Michelangelo, and the Beatles are not impossible to assimilate (though in some sense they might have assimilated us).

A number of years ago, a local radio station in Chicago, where I lived, had a feature called "Make It or Break It," in which the host would play a new song and ask members of the audience to call in to say if they liked what they heard. After they said that they liked it, the host would ask: "Why?" The usual answer was, "I like the way it sounds!" Exasperated by that answer, the host stopped asking for an explanation.

I asked ChatGPT to write the first paragraph of a bestselling novel. Here's what it produced:

The sun had set hours ago, casting a warm glow over the small town of Millfield as the last of its residents settled into their homes for the night. In a secluded corner of the town, a young woman sat on her porch, her eyes fixed on the star-filled sky above. She had lived in Millfield all her life, and yet she still felt as if there was something missing, a sense of longing that she couldn't quite place. Little did she know, her life was about to change in ways she could have never imagined.

That isn't horrible, but it's pretty formulaic. Could a novel with that start turn out to be a spectacular success? Sure. But compare this:

It was a bright cold day in April, and the clocks were striking thirteen.

That is the first paragraph of George Orwell's *1984*, and it is very good indeed. What makes it very good is that it starts out formulaic, and then it delivers a kick. Any book can start, "It was a bright cold day in April." But the clocks striking thirteen? What is that about? True, the book could turn out to be awful, but the predictable start, followed by a kick and a mystery, is hard to resist. Or consider this, from Mark Twain's *Adventures of Huckleberry Finn*:

You don't know about me without you have read a book by the name of The Adventures of Tom Sawyer; but that ain't no matter. That book was made by Mr. Mark Twain, and he told the truth, mainly. There was things which he stretched, but mainly he told the truth. That is nothing. I never seen anybody but lied one time or another, without it was Aunt Polly, or the widow, or maybe Mary. Aunt Polly—Tom's Aunt Polly, she is—and Mary, and the Widow Douglas is all told about in that book, which is mostly a true book, with some stretchers, as I said before.

Twain is having a lot of fun here, and the fun is infectious. ("Mr. Mark Twain," Huck says.) The book we are reading was also written by Twain, of course, but he makes us suspend our disbelief, and to think in some part of our minds, that we are now reading something by Huckleberry Finn. We think that in part because Huck's voice is authentic, and in part because Huck is credible, confiding in us that Twain "told the truth, mainly." "I never seen anybody but lied one time or another," Huck allows. Of course, the whole paragraph is fiction, which adds to the fun. Twain is full of tricks. His real name was Samuel Clemens, so we are speaking of mirrors within mirrors.

If you look at various lists—the bestselling books of all time, the bestselling albums of all time, the highest-grossing films of all time—you are unlikely to be shocked. Table 4-1, for example, shows the highest-grossing films, adjusted for inflation.

In one or another way, all of them are terrific. But notably, they are terrific in very different ways; nothing seems to unite them. *Jaws* and *The Exorcist* are scary; the others are not. *Gone with the Wind, The Sound of Music,* and *Doctor Zhivago* are romantic; the others are not. And of the ten, only *Gone with the Wind* and *Star Wars* make the critics' lists. *Casablanca,* the most romantic and

TABLE 4-1

Highest-grossing films

1	*Gone with the Wind*	1939
2	*Star Wars: Episode IV — A New Hope*	1977
3	*The Sound of Music*	1965
4	*E.T. the Extra-Terrestrial*	1982
5	*Titanic*	1997
6	*The Ten Commandments*	1956
7	*Jaws*	1975
8	*Doctor Zhivago*	1965
9	*The Exoricist*	1973
10	*Snow White and the Seven Dwarfs*	1937

best movie of all time (in my view, and I am not the only one), is not close to the highest-grossing movie of all time.

In the abstract, it is not easy to say all that much about quality. Particulars are essential. But we can say that what is true of music is true of many things: excessive familiarity is boring, and excessive novelty is incomprehensible. Stephen King is a case in point. He uses a lot of familiar tropes, but he delivers plenty of shocks, and he offers an unlikely combination of warmth, melancholy, and edge. At his best, he is elegiac.

Bob Dylan is also a case in point. He borrows a great deal, and he has often been accused of plagiarism. (Something similar might be said, by the way, about Martin Luther King Jr.) Hearing Dylan, people hear, in a sense, what they have heard before, but he adds something new and jarring, even thrilling.

Let's turn now to some particulars. Any selection of cases will, of course, have a high degree of randomness to it. I begin with the case of Romantic literature, simply because it is so vivid and has been so well-documented. I then turn to a selection of iconic works or people that I particularly love (*Star Wars*, Bob Dylan, Stan Lee, the Beatles) or that seem to me especially striking and that I know something about (Ayn Rand, the once-famous Witch of Lime Street). It will be obvious that my selections are arbitrary and highly personal, even idiosyncratic. If there is a unifying characteristic in my selections, it is that all of them have a kind of infectious exuberance. Apparently I like that.

Whether or not you do, my hope is that the examples help to illustrate my main points here. I also hope that my enthusiasm for (most of) my subjects, and their extraordinary talents, will not get in the way of an appreciation of the role of serendipity's black box in vaulting them to the positions that they ended up occupying. At times, we will open up that black box and see what we can find there.

PART TWO
Icons

CHAPTER 5

"Stolen, Stolen
Be Your Apples"

H ave you heard of Leigh Hunt? I was an English major
in college, but I confess that until recently, I had not.
A friend drew my attention to him. Here's his poem
"Jenny Kiss'd Me":

Jenny kiss'd me when we met,
Jumping from the chair she sat in;
Time, you thief, who love to get
Sweets into your list, put that in!
Say I'm weary, say I'm sad,
Say that health and wealth have miss'd me,
Say I'm growing old, but add,
Jenny kiss'd me.[1]

It's good, isn't it? It is funny and high-spirited, and it says something true about memory, love, and romance. You might be weary
and sad, and you might be sick and poor and old, but if Jenny kissed

you, well then. Here's another poem by Hunt, more complicated and a bit edgier:

> We, the Fairies, blithe and antic,
> Of dimensions not gigantic,
> Though the moonshine mostly keep us,
> Oft in orchards frisk and peep us.
>
> Stolen sweets are always sweeter,
> Stolen kisses much completer,
> Stolen looks are nice in chapels,
> Stolen, stolen, be your apples.
>
> When to bed the world are bobbing,
> Then's the time for orchard-robbing;
> Yet the fruit were scarce worth peeling,
> Were it not for stealing, stealing.[2]

That is better than good, isn't it? "Stolen looks are nice in chapels"—that is not the most obvious thing to say, and it's a bit shocking. (Romance and also a hint of sex, in chapels?) But stolen looks really are nice in chapels; it's true. (Isn't it?) In his time, Hunt was celebrated as one of the greatest poets in the English language. He was thought to be much better than John Keats. What happened? We will get there.

How can social dynamics help to explain the success of cultural figures? Of poets, novelists, and musicians? Does randomness matter? For John Milton, William Wordsworth, and Joni Mitchell? If so, what does randomness mean, exactly? These are difficult questions to answer. To do so, we would need to specify the hypotheses we mean to test, and then we would need to test them. We have seen that the category of social influences is large and diverse; it includes not only initial popularity, but also prominent reviewers, well-known or wealthy sponsors, networks, fans, perceived identity (Do young people like x or y? Do rebellious people like x or y?), and conventions of form, which will vary over time and place. It will also include fit, or misfit, with local or contemporary concerns and preoccupations. In one nation, Milton, Wordsworth, and Mitchell might resonate immediately, because they build on, or perhaps deliver an intriguing shock to, something that is liked and familiar. In another nation, one or all might be barely intelligible.

The Music Lab experiment was able to test a clear hypothesis: Would the popularity of songs be affected by social influences, so that download rankings would vary across subgroups? To undertake a comparable test, we might identify a set of novelists (say, Thomas Hardy, Charles Dickens, Jane Austen, James Joyce, George Orwell, A. S. Byatt, Joyce Carol Oates, Stephen King, and Harlan Coben), treat them like songs, and see whether groups, in conditions like those in the Music Lab experiment, would produce similar rankings. It would certainly be possible to do something like that with unknown novelists.

It would be much harder to do that with famous novelists, or to see how they might be compared to lesser-known novelists, either in their times or ours. Those who are already famous have a big advantage. History is not a randomized controlled experiment; it is run only once. For that reason, it is not easy to know how we might test the role and importance of social influences (and other factors) with respect to well-known poets, novelists, musicians, and the like, or even to specify the hypothesis we are testing (a point to which I will return).

Nonetheless, H. J. Jackson's stunning study of literary reputation offers important clues, and it strongly suggests that accident, contingency, champions, and luck play a massive role.[3] You can easily see her work as strong evidence in support of the claim that intrinsic merit is not enough for enduring fame, even over generations. You can also take her findings to be a strong rebuttal to Samuel Johnson's faith in the test of time. Those whom we now most celebrate from the Romantic period benefited from posthumous champions, from informational cascades, and from group polarization. Those whom we do *not* celebrate did not benefit from those things (and they might be every bit as great as those we do celebrate).

Jackson explores, among other things, the twists and turns that led to the canonization of William Wordsworth, John Keats, Jane Austen, and William Blake, and the contrastingly lower(ed) reputations of George Crabbe, Robert Southey, Barry Cornwall, Hunt, and Mary Brunton. In a sense, Jackson can be read to make the provocative argument that over a much longer time scale, Wordsworth, Keats, Austen, and Blake were like successful songs in the Music Lab study, and that Crabbe, Southey, Cornwall, Hunt, and Brunton were akin to the unsuccessful ones. Are the Beatles in some respects like Keats? Are the Kinks in some respects like Hunt? We will get to that.

In terms of perceived quality, Jackson finds that Keats, Cornwall, and Hunt were grouped together during their lifetimes. The same is true of Wordsworth, Crabbe, and Southey, and also of Austen and Brunton. If one asked their contemporaries which names, of these eight, would be most famous in the twenty-first century, there would be no consensus in favor of Keats, Wordsworth, and Austen. In particular, Jackson notes that Keats may well count, here and now, as the most beloved English language poet of all time—but at the time of his death, he believed that he had utterly failed in his somewhat desperate quest for literary fame. He said that he would "sooner fail than not be among the greatest."⁴ But in his view, he had not come close to succeeding.

Keats abandoned his long poems, even though he believed that lasting fame could only be obtained through such poems. Indeed, he left instructions that his gravestone have no name, but only these pathetic words: "Here lies one whose name was writ in water."⁵ In Keats's time, Cornwall was far more successful; he was regarded as the great poet while Keats was met with something closer to indifference or hostility.

Jackson poses a hypothetical: If Cornwall had died young (and he was in poor health much of his life), and if Keats had managed to survive, might we not be quoting Cornwall ("O power of love so fearful and so fair") rather than Keats ("A thing of beauty is a joy

John Keats

Source: John Keats. Wood engraving after W. Hilton, 1872 via Creative Commons Attribution 4.0. Courtesy of Wellcome Library, London.

forever")? Jackson points to the "conundrum of Barry Cornwall's success with the same audience that spurned Keats."[6]

Tracing Keats's improbable rise to prominence decades after his death, Jackson writes, "It seems that his reputation was dependent less on the efforts of particular individuals than on groups, overlapping networks of like-minded acquaintances starting up on a small scale, the collective chatter that later becomes the buzz of fame."[7] (Informational cascades, reputational cascades, network effects, and group polarization are all relevant here.) Various things had to happen—and they did.

In the decades after his death, a small number of influential friends, including Hunt and Cornwall themselves, testified to his greatness.[8] People started to like short poems, not just long ones. Serendipitously, his work made its way into collections and anthologies. In most of those volumes, Keats was not featured prominently, but in 1829, a prominent publisher in France grouped him with Shelley and Coleridge.[9]

That edition turned out to be important to Keats's rise; it was reprinted in the United States, and thus gave him a reputation there that he did not have in England. Tennyson loved Keats, and as Tennyson's reputation grew, so did Keats's.[10] From 1846 to 1880, a publisher named Edward Moxon published separate volumes of Keats's *Poetical Works*, with new illustrations and introductions. In 1848, Moxon published a biography of Keats by Richard Monckton Milnes; the biography had a major effect on Keats's reputation.[11] Intriguingly, Milnes described Keats as a tragic figure, one with great potential that had never been realized; "no one doubts," he wrote, "that a true genius was suddenly arrested, and they who will not allow him to have won his place in the first ranks of English poets will not deny the promise of his candidature."[12]

Nonetheless, Milnes characterized Keats as an "original genius."[13] He provided a gripping narrative of a life cut short. Keats's own nature—was he sensitive, sickly, effeminate?—produced a kind of intrigue that has fascinated readers for centuries. Under the influence of Moxon and Milnes, Keats's work obtained a larger place in collections and anthologies, and by 1857, Keats was described in the *Encylopedia Brittanica* as one of the two or three most popular poets of his generation.[14] In 1861, eleven of Keats's poems were included in Palgrave's *The Golden Treasury*.[15]

By the end of the nineteenth century, Keats had become iconic, with one influential writer declaring, "Every critic of modern English poetry is of necessity a critic of Keats."[16] Pause over that. And by the early twentieth century, Keats was in the pantheon; he had become our Keats.

Jackson does not deny Keats's genius. But in terms of pure poetic quality, she urges, Cornwall's virtues and vices greatly overlap with those of Keats.[17] Jackson's remarkable conclusion, which she makes quite plausible, is that "as far as reputation is concerned, the differences between them are largely personal and accidental."[18] At the very least, it is necessary to come to terms with the "conundrum of Barry Cornwall's success with the same audience that spurned Keats."[19]

And then there is the question of Leigh Hunt. While their contemporaries put Cornwall far above Keats, Hunt was ranked above them both.[20] And if we are interested in professional opinions, we will find that Wordsworth, Samuel Taylor Coleridge, and Lord Byron all ranked Cornwall highest of the three.[21] Shelley liked Hunt the best.[22] As Jackson puts it:

An overview of the history of the reception of Wordsworth's work offers little support for his theory of the autonomous isolated genius who generates works of overwhelming intrinsic merit and wins readers over one at a time until the enlightened audience achieves critical mass. On the contrary, it reveals a process of regular reinterpretation involving, at every turn, the vital initiative of other agents.[23]

In fact, Jackson offers a "scorecard," one that, in her telling, helps account for lasting fame.[24] At the top are four factors:

- Threshold quality

- Threshold quantity

- Champions (including societies, descendants, keepers of the flame, and individual advocates)

- Biography

For our purposes here, the most important of these are quality and champions; the additions of quantity and biography are intriguing. Jackson also points to other factors, including:

- The number of copies in circulation

- Critical tradition

- Visualizability

- Locatability (tourism and shrine, for example)

- Adaptation

- Variety of audience

- Anthology

- Reference books

- Education system

- Higher education

- Controversy

- Celebrity endorsements

It's a useful list, building on the rise and fall of Jackson's literary figures. But we have to offer two cautionary notes. First: To make progress, we would need to know what on the list is necessary, what is important, what is useful, and what is important or useful but not necessary. If we knew that, we might be able to simplify Jackson's scorecard in various ways, emphasizing that many of the items are vehicles by which cascades can occur and spread. Still, it is important to see the sheer heterogeneity of the vehicles.

Second: Beware of sampling on the dependent variable! Many people are included in anthologies, but they do not end up with posthumous fame. Many people are part of controversies, but fame eludes them. Many people receive celebrity endorsements, but celebrity endorsements are just about all that they receive. Quality and quantity are not enough. It is plausible to think that Jackson has pointed to contributing factors and also to a few factors that might be necessary, or at least close to it (Quality? Champions?), but there is no how-to manual here.[25]

The System Did Not Work

It is tempting, of course, to say that history should be seen as a market, and that ultimate success went to the best. On this view, the system worked. But perhaps not. How would we know, exactly? Jackson is critical of the idea that we prefer Wordsworth and Austen to Southey and Brunton because "they are immeasurably better writers, the authors of masterpieces."[26] In her account, "no more than threshold competence—a relatively low standard of merit—has ever been necessary to keep a writer's works in favor."[27]

Emphasizing the rivalry among Cornwall, Hunt, and Keats, she notes that the former "ranked much higher in the public estimation than" Keats did "in their day."[28] Tracing Keats's rise and the fall of Cornwall and Hunt, she seeks to show "how small a part merit plays in the process of recognition and reward."[29] In terms of changing reputations over time, Jackson places a particular emphasis on echo chamber effects, which can consolidate a writer's image.[30] Group polarization greatly mattered to Keats's ascendancy.

Mary Brunton published *Self-Control*, a novel, in 1811.[31] No fewer than three editions appeared in that year, and a fourth followed in 1812.[32] The novel was energetic and even thrilling. It dealt with a fatal love affair, in which a seventeen-year-old woman, Laura Montreville, refuses a dramatic proposal from the wealthy and charming Colonel Hargrave, a rake: elope with him and become his mistress. Ultimately Hargrave kidnaps her. She escapes.

Believing that he has driven her to her death, Hargrave kills himself. Laura marries a steady and proper (and self-controlled) gentleman instead. The last sentence of the novel puts it simply: "The joys that spring from chastened affection, tempered desires, useful employment, and devout meditation, must be felt—they cannot be described."[33] The novel works because it flirts with scandal, and encourages the reader to be thrilled by it—and then patiently insists on a commitment to the joys of a dutiful, scandal-free life. Talk about having your cake and eating it too. And what a good title!

Self-Control was a terrific success, and Brunton followed it in short order with another novel, *Discipline*, published in 1815; it also did extremely well.[34] She had an assortment of plans for future writing, but she died in 1818 after giving birth to a stillborn child.[35] For almost a half-century, Brunton continued to be read and admired, and by most measures, she stood above Jane Austen, her contemporary. In reference books about English literature, Brunton received more attention than Austen.[36]

But, of course, Brunton's work has faded into obscurity, while Austen has become a giant. Why was that? In Jackson's account, Brunton faced a number of challenges.[37] She and her husband had no children. Her work lacked a champion. She had no connection to publishers. Her work was a bit racier than Austen's, and so was not likely to be read by children. She herself did not seek fame or seek to cultivate it. For reasons that remain a bit mysterious, she never obtained enthusiastic support from critics or publishers. In a way, she was literature's Robert Johnson—but in reverse.

The puzzle is that by 1860, Brunton and Austen had similar careers. Brunton died in 1818 at the age of forty; Austen died in 1817 at the age of forty-two. Austen had written more; Brunton had been better received. The two learned a great deal from each other's work. Austen was certainly influenced by Brunton. Some contemporary readers were unable to distinguish between them.[38] Jackson urges, and makes it plausible to think, that what "happened to Brunton—the gradual fading and extinction of her name—could easily have happened to Austen."[39] If we go back to the 1860s, that might even have seemed inevitable. But Austen has of course entered the pantheon.

The reason is her extraordinary *posthumous* career. That career was not "a straight-line history. It's not an account best laid out with a single overarching argument."[40] It is instead a fascinating tale with diverging themes and intriguingly different "Aunt Janes": the

Jane Austen

Source: *J. Austen*, Johnson Wilson & Co., Publishers, 1873.

cheerful, pious aunt, kind and generous to all; the romantic; the traditionalist; the cynic about romance; the chronicler of patriarchy; the committed conservative; the unflinching progressive; the fierce defender of female independence; the originator of girl-power feminism. The vision any group has of Jane Austen tells us much more about that group than it does about her. In any event, she is now "a household name, with greater recognition than any other author writing in England not named William Shakespeare."[41] By the late nineteenth century, she became known as the Shakespeare of Prose."[42]

How did that happen? In the leading account, Austen's reputation "was created almost entirely posthumously, first by her siblings, familial descendants, and a few reviewers, involving what we'd now call celebrity endorsements, logrolling quotes, trash talk, commercial efforts, and enthusiast activities."[43] Is there an Austen cult? Absolutely. In fact, there are plenty of them.

A key moment was the publication in 1870 of *A Memoir of Jane Austen*, by James Austen-Leigh (Austen's nephew). The book was effectively a production of the Austen family, including cousins.[44] Its first sentence set the tone: "More than half a century has passed away since I, the youngest of the mourners, attended the funeral of my dear aunt Jane in Winchester Cathedral; and now, in my old age, I am asked whether my memory will serve to rescue from oblivion any events of her life or any traits of her character to satisfy the enquiries of a generation of readers who have been born since she died."

For reasons that remain unclear, *Memoir* sold well and received a large number of reviews. It gave a face to the novelist, and a sense of her personality, and in Jackson's account, "made her an object of idolization," and turned out to be "the origin of the cult."[45] It was also full of speculations and distortions, making Austen seem a lot like a character in her novels. In Austen-Leigh's account, Austen was a genius, and an unfairly neglected one. But she was not to be neglected for long.

In 1832, the copyrights to all six of Austen's novels were purchased by a publisher named Richard Bentley. For decades, Bentley was in charge of Austen's legacy.[46] In 1833, Bentley published a collected edition of the novels, including ten remarkable illustrations, which were widely circulated. Bentley's Austen titles were republished frequently, and her readership showed slow but steady growth.[47] Between 1870 and 1893, Austen's work started to receive far greater attention and acclaim, especially among young readers, for whom it was deemed suitable.

In the late nineteenth century, publishers took the bait, with numerous illustrations of scenes from the novels, enabling readers (and nonreaders) to visualize Austen's characters.[48] Starting in the 1890s and possibly earlier, Austen's plays were dramatized; her work became a significant presence on the stage, reaching its highest levels of commercial success in the 1930s.[49] The Jane Austen Society was founded in 1940.[50] The rest, as they say, is history.

As Jackson sees it, "the process by which she outstripped other novelists of her age depended on less obvious factors, most of them extraneous to the works themselves."[51] Could Brunton have a revival? Jackson raises the possibility that "one blockbuster movie or mainstream television series might do the trick."[52]

A True Poet

Do you know William Blake? His poem "Jerusalem" is carved on my soul. In my high school, we sang the poem every week:

And did those feet in ancient time
Walk upon Englands mountains green:
And was the holy Lamb of God,
On Englands pleasant pastures seen!

And did the Countenance Divine,
Shine forth upon our clouded hills?
And was Jerusalem builded here,
Among these dark Satanic Mills?

Bring me my Bow of burning gold:
Bring me my arrows of desire:

Bring me my Spear: O clouds unfold!
Bring me my Chariot of fire!

I will not cease from Mental Fight,
Nor shall my sword sleep in my hand:
Till we have built Jerusalem,
In Englands green & pleasant Land.[53]

Even without the music, that is stirring. And schoolchildren in
many nations know this exceedingly complicated one:

Tyger Tyger, burning bright,
In the forests of the night;
What immortal hand or eye,
Could frame thy fearful symmetry?

In what distant deeps or skies.
Burnt the fire of thine eyes?
On what wings dare he aspire?
What the hand, dare seize the fire?

And what shoulder, & what art,
Could twist the sinews of thy heart?
And when thy heart began to beat.
What dread hand? & what dread feet?

What the hammer? what the chain,
In what furnace was thy brain?
What the anvil? what dread grasp.
Dare its deadly terrors clasp?

When the stars threw down their spears
And water'd heaven with their tears:
Did he smile his work to see?
Did he who made the Lamb make thee?

Tyger Tyger burning bright,
In the forests of the night:
What immortal hand or eye,
Dare frame thy fearful symmetry?[54]

Blake had so much to say. Consider this Proverb of Hell: "Sooner murder an infant in its cradle than nurse unacted desires." Or this: "The road of excess leads to the palace of wisdom. Prudence is a rich ugly old maid courted by Incapacity. He who desires but acts not, breeds pestilence."

Here are Blake's words on Milton's *Paradise Lost*, the greatest religious poem in the English language: "The reason Milton wrote in fetters when he wrote of Angels & God, and at liberty when of Devils & Hell, is because he was a true Poet and of the Devil's party without knowing it." Or consider this observation about Sir Joshua Reynolds, who praised generalization: "To Generalize is to be an Idiot. To Particularize is the Alone Distinction of Merit."

Blake mined the depths of the human soul. But in his lifetime, he was obscure; his works "were almost unknown to his contemporaries."[55] If he was known as anything, it was as an engraver.[56] His poetry might have been known to a handful of people. After his wife died in 1831, it looked as if his works *might not survive at all*.[57] From 1827 to 1863, Blake received little attention. He came before the public thirty years after his death, through an unlikely biography whose revealing subtitle was *"Pictor Ignotus": The Unknown Painter*.[58] The biography, written by Alexander Gilchrist and still widely admired, celebrated Blake as an artist and as a poet. Gilchrist offered extensive quotations from Blake's writing; Blake was thus a beneficiary of a highly improbable and complex recovery project, barely rescuing him from literary oblivion.

Gilchrist himself put it this way: "From nearly all collections of beauties of 'The English Poets,' catholic to demerit as these are, tender of the expired and expiring reputations, one name has been perseveringly exiled."[59] Gilchrist sought to bring Blake out of exile. He was evidently excited by the unpopularity of the work that he sought to celebrate. A second volume, compiled by Gilchrist and others, contained long extracts from Blake's work. Apparently as a result, interest in Blake increased, and volumes of his poetry began to appear. From 1863 until the First World War, Blake enjoyed a spectacular recovery.[60] And from 1940 until 1968, there was a second Blake revival, when he "was resurrected as an icon of youthful radicalism."[61]

Romance

I have noted that the Matthew Effect ends up altering what we like and appreciate. Sounding a lot like Samuel Johnson on Shakespeare, Jackson writes, "Success reinforces and magnifies merit. Over time, winners . . . change the rules. They become benchmarks. Their own work is sifted, and the work of others is measured by reference to the qualities in the handful of poems that are thought to be their best."[62]

By what criteria do we evaluate literature, music, or art? The answer might well be established by the very work that has emerged as iconic. If we test Keats, Hunt, and Cornwall by the criteria that Keats's ascendancy has established, of course we will choose Keats. But does that mean that Keats is better? It is worth pausing over this point. Those who become ascendant, perhaps as a result of something like accident, affect tastes and values, and for that very reason, their continued ascendancy might be assured— not because they are better, but because the standard has been established by what they did. (It is a little like romance. Actually it is a lot like romance. If you love someone, others might fall short to you, not necessarily because they really fall short, but because they fall short by reference to the standards established by the person who preceded them.)

Jackson's conclusion is that notwithstanding "the common assumption that over time, the best writers come out on top, the reception histories . . . show that long-term survival has depended more on external circumstances and accidental advantages than on inherent literary worth."[63] In her view, Keats does not have more inherent merit than Hunt and Cornwall.[64] Perhaps the most famous literary figures are, in fact, greater than those who are unknown; we would be strongly inclined to think so. How could we not? We grew up with them. But perhaps we are wrong, A modest suggestion is that with a little push or shove, or download equivalents at the right time, the literary canon could feature Crabbe, Hunt, and Brunton.[65] And here's Hunt one more time:

> Stolen sweets are always sweeter,
> Stolen kisses much completer,
> Stolen looks are nice in chapels,
> Stolen, stolen, be your apples.[66]

Did Keats write better lines than those?

CHAPTER 6

The Force

Right out of the gate, *Star Wars* (now known as *A New Hope*) was a spectacular hit. On its opening day, May 27, 1977, it was shown in just thirty-two theaters, but it broke records for nine of them, including four of the five New York theaters in which it was screened.[1] Even though the movie premiered on a Wednesday, its single-day total was $254,809, or $8,000 per location.[2] At Mann's Chinese Theatre, in Hollywood, the single-day total alone was $19,358, while Manhattan's Astor Plaza brought in $20,322.[3]

True, it did not quite win the box-office sweepstakes on its opening weekend; *Smokey and the Bandit* did that, earning $2.7 million to $2.5 million for *Star Wars*.[4] But the immortal *Smokey* was shown on a whopping 386 screens, and with a grand weekend total of 43, *Star Wars* didn't have much of a chance.[5]

The movie continued to be a sensation throughout the summer. Entire towns mobilized, seemingly en masse, in order to see it. Within a few months of its release, fully half of the population of Benton County, Oregon, had seen the film.[6] As the amazement and exhilaration spread, its popularity grew in its initial months, finally peaking in mid-August, when it was showing at approximately eleven hundred theaters across the country.[7] Its appeal sustained itself over time. Some forty-two theaters screened the movie continuously for over a year.[8] Across the United States, theaters were forced to order new prints because the old ones were literally being worn out.[9]

Of course, *Star Wars* was a smashing financial success. By September, it had become Twentieth Century Fox's most successful film ever.[10] As a direct result of the movie's performance, the studio's stock skyrocketed: it jumped from $6 a share to nearly $27 a share in the immediate aftermath of the movie's release.[11] In just a few months, *Star Wars* surpassed *Jaws* to become the highest-grossing film of all time.[12] When its first theatrical run finally ended, it had made $307 million.[13]

That's 240 percent of the earnings of the second-highest grossing film of 1977, *Close Encounters of the Third Kind*, which earned $128 million.[14] It's also roughly six times the earnings of the year's fifth-highest earner, *A Bridge Too Far*—which brought in $50.8 million—and approximately eighteen times the earnings of *Kingdom of the Spiders*, which came in tenth at the box office with $17 million.[15] If we include its rereleases and adjust for ticket price inflation, *Star Wars* has made an estimated $1.63 billion at the box office.[16]

By way of comparison, this number exceeds *Avatar*'s adjusted earnings by over $600 million.[17] In terms of GDP, it trumps Samoa by about $700 million.[18] In inflation-adjusted earnings, only *Gone with the Wind* tops *Star Wars*, and they're not that far apart. *A New Hope* is comfortably ahead of *The Sound of Music*, *E.T.*, *Titanic*, *The Ten Commandments*, and *Jaws*.

The five Lucas sequels and prequels also enjoyed terrific levels of success. *The Empire Strikes Back* went on to make $209 million during its first box-office run, and all of the later Lucas films made well over $200 million in their initial theatrical releases.[19] *The Phantom Menace* is probably the worst of the lot, but of the two Lucas trilogies, it had the highest unadjusted gross. Once you adjust for inflation (as you should), it still ranks an impressive nineteenth of all time, just two spots below *Return of the Jedi* and six below *The Empire Strikes Back*.[20]

These are just numbers, of course. In terms of the culture, the figures don't come close to capturing the impact of the series. Around the world, presidents know about it, and so do senators and Supreme Court justices, and so does your kid, and so do your parents. If you want to bond with someone you don't know, try talking about *Star Wars*. It's a lot better than the weather, and it's likely to work.

"A Load of Rubbish"

But there's an irony here, and a major puzzle too. In the early stages, Lucas reports, "nobody thought that it was going to be a big hit."[21] When *Star Wars* was released, a lot of insiders thought that they had a dud on their hands. Throughout its production, there was "basic apathy toward the project with Fox," and many executives had "little faith in the film or its director."[22] Wild but true: they "hoped a lot of times that it would just go away."[23]

It's revealing that when Lucas and his team started to run out of cash, Lucas had to pay directly out of the money he had made from his earlier movie, *American Graffiti* (which was also a wholly unanticipated hit).[24] Without that infusion of personal cash, the whole project might well have collapsed. Nor was the near-universal negativity solely a product of trepidation about the unusual nature of the whole project. (Droids? The Force? Some old guy named Obi-Wan? Played by Alec Guinness? Lightsabers?) After the board at Fox finally saw a rough cut, there was "no applause, not even a smile. We were really depressed."[25]

Even during the last stages, Lucas himself "didn't think the film was going to be successful."[26] Most people at the studio agreed; "the board didn't have any faith in it."[27] As evidence of its lack of faith, the studio saw fit to show just one winter trailer for the film, at Christmas; it was shown only once more, during Easter.

Astonishingly, Fox seemed to think that the movie wasn't even worth the celluloid on which it was printed—literally. The studio made fewer than one hundred prints, which caused a terrible problem once the crowds demanded to see it.[28] Far more optimistic than most, Lucas himself projected that because young people might like it, it could earn $16 million, about as much as the average Disney movie.[29] He claimed that the chances of its doing much better than that were "a zillion to one."[30]

Even after its smashing success, Lucas said, "I expected to break even on it, I still can't understand it."[31] His then-wife and close collaborator, Marcia Lucas, thought that Martin Scorsese's *New York, New York* (which she also helped edit) would do better.[32]

For their part, movie theaters, whose business is to know what people will like, responded very cautiously. Fox hoped for advance guarantees of $10 million but got only a fraction of that: a humiliating $1.5 million. Its most promising film of the summer, it thought, was *The Other Side of Midnight*, and to coerce interest in Lucas's film, the studio warned theaters that if they didn't take *Star Wars*, they wouldn't get that film, either.

The whole marketing enterprise might have collapsed if not for the tireless efforts of Charley Lippincott, a friend of Lucas, who had lot of faith in the movie. Lippincott promoted it aggressively and helped to get it into those admittedly paltry thirty-two theaters—one of which was the prestigious and large Coronet in San Francisco. As it turned out, his success with the Coronet really mattered.

Immediately after *Star Wars* opened, Lucas and his wife went on vacation in Hawaii. They wanted to be far away not only because they wanted a vacation, but also because as the reviews came in, they feared that Lucas "had just released a flop."[33] In remote Hawaii they could escape what "Lucas was certain was going to be a disaster."[34] In 2015, he reported that even his friends "didn't have any faith in it either. And the [studio] board didn't have any faith in it. . . . Nobody liked it."[35]

The actors agreed. Anthony Daniels (C-3PO) said, "There was a general atmosphere on the set that we were making a complete turkey."[36] Harrison Ford noted, "There's this giant guy in a dog suit walking around. It was ridiculous."[37] David Prowse, who played Darth Vader (though of course James Earl Jones did the all-important voice), noted, "Most of us thought we were filming a load of rubbish."[38] Mark Hamill observed, "I remember thinking, it's really hard to keep a straight face doing this stuff. Alec Guinness sitting next to a Wookiee—what's wrong with this picture?"[39] Years afterward, Carrie Fisher recalled, "The film wasn't supposed to do what it did—nothing was supposed to do that."[40]

The sound designer, Ben Burtt, thought the movie might be a success for a few weeks: "The best I could imagine was that we would get to have a table at next year's Star Trek convention."[41] Even after the massive opening crowds, Lucas said, "Science fiction films get this little group of sci-fi fans. They'll come to anything in the first week. Just wait."[42] As one film scholar summarized the evidence, "no one predicted" the critical admiration and viewer fanaticism that followed release of *Star Wars*.[43]

Return to the Music Lab. Why didn't anyone see what was coming? Aren't movie studios, and the experts who staff them, supposed to be good at that sort of thing?

Quality

After its release, *Star Wars* was, of course, immediately recognized as something special. No explanation of its success can disregard that fact. In fact, a few people liked it in advance. We have seen that Fox executives were ambivalent or negative, but one of them, Gareth Wigan, cried during a limited screening and concluded that *Star Wars* was "the greatest film [he'd] ever seen."[44] At an advance screening a few weeks later, Steven Spielberg immediately labeled it "the greatest movie ever made."[45]

Audience interest exploded early on, which suggests that people's appreciation of its amazingness, rather than social influences, was the spark. In its first screening for the general public, the audience started cheering at the beginning—and stopped only as the credits rolled.[46] At the Coronet, which Lippincott had worked so hard to book, lines circled the block. Its manager described the scene as follows: "Old people, young people, children, Hare Krishna groups. They bring cards to play in line. We have checker players, we have chess players; people with paint and sequins on their faces. Fruit eaters like I've never seen before, people loaded on grass and LSD."[47]

At the Avco Theater in Los Angeles, the manager reported that he had to turn away five thousand people over Memorial Day weekend. And before would-be attendees could even begin to navigate the lines, they often had to contend with standstill traffic around urban theaters that effectively shut down driving as a way of getting to a show.[48]

In general, the initial reviews were exceedingly positive, and in some cases they were rapturous. Influential *New York Times* film critic Vincent Canby labeled the film "the most elaborate, most expensive, most beautiful movie serial ever made."[49] A spectacular review in the *San Francisco Chronicle* described it as "the most visually awesome" work since *2001: A Space Odyssey*, while also praising it as "intriguingly human in its scope and boundaries."[50] Joseph Gelmis of *Newsday* went further still, crowning *Star Wars* as "one of the greatest adventure movies ever made" and a "masterpiece of entertainment."[51]

Popular magazines ran stories not only on the movie but also on the phenomenon. "Every TV show news program had done a segment on the crowds waiting to see this amazing movie."[52] At that year's Academy Awards, *Star Wars* was nominated in

Yoda

Source: Yoda Fountain, via Creative Commons Attribution-ShareAlike 2.0. Courtesy of SW77 on FLICKR.

no fewer than eleven categories, including Best Picture. It came away with seven victories.[53] Decades later, numerous directors recall seeing the film and being (to use the technical term) blown away.

Ridley Scott said that he felt "so inspired [he] wanted to shoot [him]self."[54] Peter Jackson said that "going to see *Star Wars* was one of the most exciting experiences that I ever had in my life."[55] Saul Zaentz—a distinguished film producer who would go on to win three Academy Awards—may have been the most moved. Taking out a page in *Variety*, he wrote an open letter to Lucas and his team, congratulating them on "giv[ing] birth to a perfect film[.] [T]he whole world will rejoice with you."[56]

For a generation, Jonathan Lethem captures the feeling this way:

In the summer of 1987 I saw *Star Wars*—the original, which is all I want to discuss here—twenty-one times. . . . But what actually occurred within the secret brackets of that experience? What emotions lurk inside that ludicrous temple of hours? What the fuck was I thinking? . . . I was always already a *Star Wars* fanatic.[57]

It's hard to top Lethem, but Todd Hansen does just that:

It was as plain as day, a truism that didn't need to be justified, an axiomatic fact of nature, that *Star Wars* was better than anything else you'd previously encountered. It was just obvious, kids didn't even need to say it to each other; it was just Known, it was Understood. And not just better, but way better: ten, twenty, times cooler than whatever the last coolest thing we'd ever seen had been. . . . It dwarfed whatever it was it had put into second place—you couldn't even see second place. Second place was somewhere off the bottom of the page.[58]

So maybe the movie was bound to succeed after all. Recall the "independent judgment" condition of the Music Lab experiment, in which people made their decisions without reference to the views of anyone else. If people saw movies in isolation, and did not learn about what others think or read reviews, there's a good chance that *Star Wars* would still have been a huge hit.

True, we'd have to ask: Under those circumstances, how would people have been able to know about the movie in the first place? But reasonable people could argue that *Star Wars* is a lot like the very top songs in the Music Lab experiment, in the sense that whatever happened in the early stages, it was going to break out. It was simply too original, too cool, too amazing.

Famous for Being Famous

Possibly so, but let's consider a different view. Some people, including Duncan Watts of the University of Pennsylvania (and coauthor of the Music Lab papers), think that essentially nothing is destined to succeed. Even the greatest work needs to benefit from adventitious circumstances, including those that produce favorable social influences. Yes, absolutely, that includes Shakespeare and da Vinci too.

For *Star Wars*, there was an informational cascade, big-time, and a reputational cascade too, and network effects helped a lot. The media can spur such cascades, and they definitely did that for George Lucas. On the very day that the movie premiered, the

Washington Post's review predicted it would be an "overwhelmingly popular" success that could "approach the phenomenal popularity of *Jaws*," which was, by some measures, the most successful movie ever at the time.[59] Just five days after its release, *Time* magazine labeled it "the year's best movie."[60]

Its success turned out to be self-perpetuating. From the opening weekend, stories about *Star Wars*' popularity, and the wild lines that it attracted, ran in news outlets throughout the country.[61] In June, *Variety* ran an article exploring how telephone operators had become overwhelmed by requests for the telephone numbers of theaters screening *Star Wars*.[62] These operators, reported *Variety*, were forced to memorize theaters' numbers when they found themselves handling a hundred calls an hour.[63]

Star Wars isn't exactly a telephone, but it benefited, and it continues to benefit, from network effects: it is one of a number of cultural goods of which people think they should be aware. Quite apart from its intrinsic merits, it's good to know about, so that you can talk to others about it. It might not be a lot of fun to stare blankly when someone makes a knowing reference to Luke Skywalker or Darth Vader, or even to Obi-Wan Kenobi. If you think that people like *Star Wars* and focus on it, you might join them for one reason above all: You don't want to be left out. You want to be part of the group.

Arion Berger notes that "it's fun to participate in some cultural swoon," and that's exactly what *Star Wars* has been.[64] Here's how Ann Friedman puts in: "Ultimately, I realized, I was going to see 'The Force Awakens' because all my friends were going to see it, and everyone else's friends were going to see it too. I was in the grip of an increasingly rare phenomenon: A true mass-cultural event."[65] As Berger notes, *Star Wars* is "simultaneously a cult artifact and a staggeringly popular phenomenon."[66] In an era of cultural fragmentation, that's a neat trick, and socially even precious. In such an era, people like it; they might even need it.

There were even literal network effects. CBS News anchor Walter Cronkite—the most trusted man in America, the nation's voice—did not ordinarily focus on movies, much less on ones that dealt with the Kessel Run and Jedi Knights. But he devoted time to *Star Wars* in the early weeks of the summer.[67] Just as in the Music Lab, initial popularity spurred additional interest.

According to J. W. Rinzler, the closest thing to the series' official biographer, the gigantic lines that continued to form for *Star Wars* throughout the summer were "fueled to a great degree by person-to-person communication."[68] In an intriguing, brisk analysis, Chris Taylor writes that while "word of mouth in the science fiction community" drew the week-one fans and "glowing reviews" produced viewers for weeks two and three, "news stories about the size of the crowds brought in the post–Memorial Day crowd."[69] That's a classic description of a cascade.

As Taylor puts it, *Star Wars* was "more than the sum of its box office. It was famous for being famous."[70] He catalogs the early network effects, on which a whole book could easily be written. People who saw the film "were familiar with funny-sounding names and catchphrases"; they "had joined an exclusive club that knew about 'the Force,' even as everyone had a different theory on what it actually was."[71]

Stephen Colbert reported that after seeing *Star Wars,* he and his friends returned to school aware that "everything was different now."[72] Ann Friedman once more: "It offers fragmented audiences a chance to remember what it feels like to be a part of something big that crosses cultural and generational lines. . . . It's nice to leave your niche and experience the truly universal once in a while."[73]

The Zeitgeist

Did *Star Wars* connect with the Zeitgeist? Did it have a special resonance for its particular time? Did Lucas, deliberately or by happenstance, end up producing what the public most wanted at that time? Is that the real reason that *Star Wars* succeeded?

A lot of people think so. In one view, the movie came at a time when the American public, traumatized by a series of demoralizing events, had an acute need for some kind of uplifting mythology. Film critic A. O. Scott captures a widely held view in insisting that the movie's success "represented what looks like the inevitable product of demographic and social forces."[74] Taylor likewise notes that, on the day of *Star Wars'* release, the Dow was at its lowest level in sixteen months, President Richard Nixon was being interviewed by David Frost, and the "fingerprints of the [Vietnam] war were everywhere."[75] For his part, theologian David Wilkinson points to the decline of the national economy, emerging ecological concerns, the fresh memories of Vietnam, the lingering dangers posed by Cold War, Watergate, and the stalling of the space program as creating a climate ripe for *Star Wars'* success.[76]

In the documentary *Star Wars: The Legacy Revealed*, journalist Linda Ellerbee notes that "it was not a hopeful time in America . . . we were cynical, we were disappointed, oil prices were through the roof, [and] our government had let us down."[77] In the words of Newt Gingrich, "the country was desperately groping for real change. *Star Wars* came around and revalidated a core mythology: that there is good and evil, and that evil has to be defeated."[78] Indeed, at a time when the president, Jimmy Carter, was taking to the air to encourage Americans to "make sacrifices" and "live thriftily," Americans might be expected to welcome a fantastic adventure a long time ago in a galaxy far, far away.[79]

But maybe not. The cultural explanation, emphasizing the Zeitgeist, might just be a way of grasping at straws. To see why this could be so, consider a little contest: In light of the unique situation of the United States in late May 1977, *Star Wars* was bound to succeed because [fill in the blank here].

You could point to the economy: the stock market, the inflation rate, the unemployment rate. You could point to the international situation: the Cold War, the Soviet Union, China, or Cuba. You could point to Watergate and its aftermath. You could speak of the civil rights movement. You could say something about technology—about the national enthusiasm and ambivalence about it. In one view, *Star Wars* spoke at once to all of those things and was bound for success for that reason.

None of these explanations can be shown to be wrong. The problem is that none of them can be shown to be right.

To see the problem, suppose that *Star Wars*, or something quite a bit like it, and with appropriate adjustments for the state of filmmaking at the time, had been released in 1959, 1969, 1989, 1999, 2009, 2019, or 2029. Would it have been a hit or a dud? Suppose that it would have been a hit. If so, smart people could have done really well on this essay contest: In light of the unique situation of the United States in late May [fill in the year], *Star Wars* was bound to succeed because [fill in the blank here]. Whatever the Zeitgeist—at least within reason—*Star Wars* could easily turn out to be a smashing success.

The upshot: whenever we say that a product succeeded because of its excellent timing, we might be right, but we might just be telling a tale, not explaining anything. The risk of the timing-was-perfect explanations is heightened for books, music, and movies, where we don't have randomized controlled trials, and where it's easy to say that success was because of an economic downturn, or an economic upturn, or a civil rights protest, or a terrorist attack. Easy— but right?

Star Wars got a lot of early help. Soon after its release, it was famous for being famous, and people wanted to see it because everyone else seemed to be seeing it. Since 1977, that's been its good fortune. *Star Wars* is a bit like the *Mona Lisa*—really famous, and much more than good, but the beneficiary of a cultural norm ("this, you have to see") that was far from inevitable. Sure, it's terrific. Sure, it resonated with the culture of the late 1970s. But it needed social influences.

CHAPTER 7

The Irresistible Stan Lee

Ll over the world, the Marvel Universe is an economic phenomenon. It is almost surreal. No fewer than six *Spider-Man* movies have hit the $300 million mark.[1] Four *Avengers* movies have done that.[2] The same is true of two *Black Panther* movies, two *Thor* movies, and three *Iron Man* movies.[3]

Astonishingly, every one of these characters sprang, at least in part, from the mind of just one person: Stan Lee. And while Lee was amazing, and so was and is Marvel, there's a Matthew Effect here, superhero-style.

To understand Lee's achievement, flash back to the early 1960s, when the world of comic books was dominated by two companies. The first was DC, home of Superman, Batman, Wonder Woman, and the Flash. The second was Marvel, home of Spider-Man, Thor, Iron Man, the Fantastic Four, the Hulk, and X-Men.

DC's superheroes were square-jawed and staid, and they tended to be serious and dull. They liked platitudes. "This looks like a job for Superman," Superman proclaimed. He also liked to announce,

"Up, up, and away" (right before he started to fly). DC's superheroes would swoop in and rescue people.

By contrast, Marvel heroes were irreverent, witty, insecure, troubled, ironic, and playful. Spider-Man called himself "Your Friendly Neighborhood Spider-Man." His nickname was "Spidey." Ben Grimm, also known as The Thing, liked to announce, "It's clobberin' time!" (right before he started to clobber). DC was Dwight Eisenhower; Marvel was John F. Kennedy. DC was Bing Crosby; Marvel was the Rolling Stones. DC was Apollo; Marvel was Dionysus.

Lee, who died in 2018 at the age of ninety-five, was Marvel's guiding spirit and its most important writer.[4] Lee helped to create an astonishing number of the company's iconic figures—Spider-Man, the Avengers, the Fantastic Four, the Hulk, the X-Men, the Black Panther, the Avengers, Thor, Daredevil (Daredevil!), Doctor Strange, Black Widow, the Silver Surfer, and Ant-Man.[5] There were many others.

Lee defined the Marvel brand. He gave readers a sense that they were in the cool kids' club—knowing, winking, rebellious, with their own private language: "Face Forward!" "Excelsior!" "'Nuff said!" I have noted that Lee created a literal fan club, known as the Merry Marvel Marching Society.[6] Lee liked alliteration, and he knew a lot about informational cascades, reputational cascades, network effects, and group polarization. He created echo chambers.

Aside from having superpowers, Lee's characters were vulnerable. You fell for them, and you felt for them. One was blind (Daredevil); another was confined to a wheelchair (Professor Xavier). By creating superheroes who faced real-world problems (romantic and otherwise), Lee channeled the insecurities of his young readers. As he put it: "The idea I had, the underlying theme, was that just because somebody is different doesn't make them better."[7] He gave that theme a political twist: "That seems to be the worst thing in human nature: We tend to dislike people who are different than we are."[8]

DC felt like the past, and Marvel felt like the future, above all because of Marvel's exuberance, sense of fun, and subversive energy. Marvel's readers felt like they were catching a wave. They felt that they were cool because they were Marvel's readers. They *were* a network, in part because they assembled themselves into one ("Avengers Assemble!"), in part because Lee made it easy for them to do that.

A personal confession: Stan Lee taught me to read. When I was a young boy in the early 1960s, I read every Marvel comic I could get. Many parents banned their children from reading comics, on the ground that they weren't "real books." But mine thought that so long as their son was reading, it didn't much matter what it was. My mother, in particular, encouraged my habit. When Thor exclaimed, "VENGEANCE IS MINE!"—well, wow. The arrival of the first issue of *Daredevil—The Man without Fear!*—was a highlight of my childhood.

In terms of cultural impact, was Lee the most important writer of the last sixty years? You could make the argument. His characters have given rise not only to numerous movies but also to television shows, plays, and novels. Countless children, and not a few adults, have identified with Bruce Banner, alter ego of the Hulk, who warned: "Mr. McGee, don't make me angry. You wouldn't like me when I'm angry."

And whatever our role in life, many of us have never forgotten Lee's line from the first Spider-Man story: "With great power there must also come—great responsibility!" If, as Shelley said, "poets are the unacknowledged legislators of the world," then Lee, the poet, was responsible for more than a few laws.[9]

Even so, Lee's reach was pretty limited for a long time. Back in the 1960s, I had a friend, about twelve years old, named Robert Levinson. Both of us loved Marvel. Rob had an idea: There should be movies about our comic book heroes! Spider-Man could have a movie; Captain America could have a movie; the Hulk could have a movie; even the Avengers could have a movie. To twelve-year-old me, Robert's idea seemed nuts. A movie about Spider-Man? Comic book heroes in movies? Of course, Rob was right. But how did all this happen?[10]

One Mighty Magazine

In the late 1950s and early 1960s, Marvel was pretty pathetic. It consisted of just one room, a tiny office in New York. The company was owned by one Martin Goodman and run by Lee, who was its only real employee, and who aspired to be a novelist. Its comic books, focusing on war, romance, and monsters, did not do well.[11] In 1957, DC offered to purchase Marvel's characters, such as they were, from the cranky Goodman, who considered the offer but declined. As Reed Tucker, chronicler of the DC-Marvel rivalry, puts it, "Imagine how different the world would be today had that deal gone through. We'll never know."[12]

It all started, really, in the summer of 1961. Born in 1922, Lee was no longer a young man; he had been with the company that would become Marvel since 1939. A mere teenager, Lee was originally asked to run errands, to proofread, and to get coffee. In 1941, he was made editor. Now pushing forty, Lee had been unsuccessful, and the comic book industry as a whole was struggling. Ashamed of his job, Lee told people that he was in "publishing" when asked what he did for a living.

In light of the economic turmoil, Goodman informed him that he could stay on as editor in chief of what was then called Atlas Comics, but he would have to fire his entire staff. Lee told a colleague, "It's like a ship sinking, and we're the rats. And we've got to get off."[13] But Lee lacked other opportunities, and he couldn't afford unemployment.

One afternoon Goodman happened to have a new idea: Lee should create a new team of superheroes, copying what DC was then doing, which was to put Superman, Batman, Wonder Woman, and Flash into a new series called Justice League. As Goodman put it, "Hey, maybe there's still a market for superheroes. Why don't you bring out a team like the Justice League?"[14] Goodman even suggested a name: the Righteous League. That sounds derivative and boring, doesn't it? Pretty much by the numbers?

Lee despised the idea; he did not think well of DC, and he did not want to mimic it. He told his wife Joanie that he wanted to quit altogether. She suggested that instead of doing that, he should think big. "If Martin wants you to create a new group of superheroes, this could be the chance for you to do it the way you've always wanted to."[15] She continued: "You could dream up plots that have more depth and substance to them, and create characters that have interesting personalities, who speak like real people." She added, "You want to quit anyway, so what's the risk?"

Lee took the bait. He never much liked Superman ("Up, up, and away!"), and he didn't want to create superheroes who were "uniform in their bland goodness." He disliked lead characters who "had only one, simple setting: swoop down, save day, retreat, repeat."[16] He also thought that women should be featured—not as anomalies like Wonder Woman, but as part of the team. With characteristic grandiosity, he decided to create "a team such as comicdom had never known."[17] He wanted them to "be fallible and feisty and, most important of all, inside their colourful, costumed booties they'd still have feet of clay."[18]

That was a wild thought, but Lee was hopeful. He enlisted Jack Kirby, one of his most brilliant artists (and today an icon in his own right), to help him to create a new kind of comic book, with flawed heroes, internal squabbles, and plenty of banter.

Lee and Kirby created something genuinely new, in the form of the Fantastic Four: Reed Richards, the too-talkative scientist, also known as Mr. Fantastic, who could elongate himself; the wise-cracking Ben Grimm, also known as the Thing, made out of stone, ugly, and absurdly strong; Susan Storm, sharp and sensible, also known as Invisible Girl, because she could disappear; and Johnny Storm, Sue's impetuous brother, also known as the Human Torch, who could turn himself into fire. (We pause only briefly over the fact that the male lead's superpower was the ability to elongate himself, and that the female lead's superpower was the ability to disappear.) On the cover of the first issue, Lee's callout box announced, "Together for the first time in one mighty magazine!"

Still, Lee didn't have high hopes. After writing it, he worried that he might get fired; his wife consoled him by saying that at least he got it out of his system.[19] But for reasons that continue to be less than clear, the team rapidly found a large, enraptured audience, with fan mail arriving in an avalanche. It was like Beatlemania. Decades later, Alan Moore, the much-celebrated comic book writer, put it this way: "I doubt you can imagine the sheer impact that single comic possessed in the comic-starved wastelands of 1961."[20] On the cover of the third issue, Lee decided to place a characteristically triumphant tagline: "The Greatest Comic Magazine in the World!!"

Why, exactly, did the Fantastic Four explode? The real answer is that we don't exactly know. It helped that it was energetic and fresh—that the superheroes were funny and human, and that they bickered. The new comic was both recognizable and something different. It was also clever. But as we have seen, that is not enough; a lot of things had to go right to trigger the tremendous sales. People had to learn about the equivalent of early downloads. They also had to learn not only that people were buying the Fantastic Four, but also that they were liking what they bought. It stands to reason that the relevant readers—mostly ages eight to eighteen—felt that they were able to join a kind of club. It appealed to their sense of identity, and their aspiration to being insiders, and being cooler-than-thou.

Because of the spectacular sales, Goodman decided to ask Lee for more. What followed was a period of astonishing creativity, with an assortment of now-iconic figures, many of them created in just two years: 1962 and 1963. After the success of the Fantastic Four, Goldman wanted another team of bickering but lovable heroes. The Righteous League this time, perhaps? But Lee didn't want to repeat himself. He responded with the Hulk, a variation on Dr. Jekyll and Mr. Hyde, with the superhero turning out to be a monster. His motto? "HULK SMASH!" (Lee was funny.) The source of the character's appeal is simple: every human being has a Hulk inside, and it can be a real struggle to keep the monster repressed.

When Lee pitched the idea of Spider-Man, a teenager bitten by a radioactive spider, he got a firm veto. Goodman noted, reasonably enough, that people hate bugs. He added that superheroes have to be adults, not teenagers. Lee persisted; he refused to give up. Without Goodman's approval, he managed to feature Spider-Man as what seemed to be a likely one-off in a series called *Amazing Fantasy*. He chose the now-legendary Steve Ditko as the artist, and Lee introduced the character with a wink: "Like costume heroes?

Confidentially, we in the comic mag business refer to them as 'long underwear characters'! And as you know, they're a dime a dozen! But we think you may find our Spiderman just a bit . . . different!" Note the dramatic ". . ." and pause if you would over Lee's "confidential" disclosure; Lee was a master of encouraging readers to think of themselves as insiders and as confidants.

Spider-Man's debut did not merely do well. It was the best-selling comic book of the decade. Stunned by the sales figures, Goodman burst into Lee's office, saying, "Stan, remember that Spider-Man idea of yours I liked so much? Why don't we turn it into a series?"[21]

Lee also helped create the X-Men: a group of young adults whose mutated genes gave them special powers. Lee's story was explicitly and intentionally about a minority group, despised because it was "different." Professor Charles Xavier, the leader of the X-Men, sought peace and mutual understanding with ordinary human beings. His nemesis was Magneto, leader of the Brotherhood of Evil Mutants, the villain of the series. Or was he? In Lee's telling, Magneto "was just trying to strike back at the people who were so bigoted and racist. He was trying to defend mutants, and because it was not treating them fairly, he decided to teach society a lesson . . . I never thought of him as a villain."[22] There is a plausible argument that Professor Xavier can be seen as a comic version of Martin Luther King Jr. and that Magneto channeled Malcolm X.

Right on the Line

Why did Lee succeed? First things first: he was funny and terrific, especially after he hit his stride in the early 1960s. That was not enough, of course. It is tempting to understand his career, and especially his spectacular creativity and success in that period, in generational terms. Lee was able to capture some of the decade's deepest commitments and ambitions. DC was stuck in the 1950s, and Lee spoke to the new dawn. Lee seemed to capture the Zeitgeist, and maybe that is why he succeeded. Maybe politics helped. In an editorial in one of his comics, he wrote:

> Let's lay it right on the line. Bigotry and racism are among the deadliest social ills plaguing the world today. But, unlike a team of costumed supervillains, they can't be halted with a punch in the snoot, or a zap from a ray gun. The only way to destroy them is to expose them—to reveal them for the insidious evils they really are. The bigot is an unreasoning hater—one who hates blindly, fanatically, indiscriminately.[23]

In response to those skeptical about political messages in comic books, Lee added, "It seems to me that a story without a message, however subliminal, is like a man without a soul. In fact, even the most escapist literature of all—old-time fairy tales and heroic legends—contained moral and philosophical points of view."[24] Lee connected directly with the culture of the time. During protests over the Vietnam War and the civil rights movement, rebellion was in the air, and Lee's defiant, wisecracking superheroes seemed to be just what the doctor ordered. As Tucker puts it, "Lee and his collaborators, whether through good sense or sheer luck, managed to introduce a different kind of hero at a time when America was entering into a period of historic social upheaval."[25]

But Lee was rarely didactic; on the contrary, he was playful and full of fun. Beyond politics, Lee channeled and in a way fueled the era's distrust of platitudes, its dynamism, its sheer exuberance. In my view, that was what made him special. It should be clear by now that this was not sufficient for his success; he also needed the magic of social influences (of which he showed a remarkable intuitive understanding; more on that soon). But Lee's exuberance was what made him unique.

The Hero with a Thousand Faces

Some people have also urged that Lee's heroes can be seen "as characters formed by the anxieties of first-generation American Jews who had fought in World War II, witnessed the Holocaust, and reflected—consciously or otherwise—on the moral obligations and complications of life after Auschwitz."[26] It's not simple to understand Lee's work this way, but we can find supporting material. Lee's birth name was Stanley Lieber. His father Jack lost his job during the Depression and spent a lot of time out of work. At the age of seventeen, Stanley was able, through family connections, to obtain an interview with Goodman, also Jewish, and a fifth-grade dropout who ran a comic book company. Lee obtained work as an errand boy.

Most of the artists and writers there were Jews, hired because they couldn't find employment elsewhere, and because most of the comic book publishers were Jewish, too. Jack Kirby, born Jacob Kurtzberg, helped create Captain America in 1941, a superhero who was obsessed with defeating the Nazis. In 1942, Lee himself enlisted in the Army. There is no question that the war against Hitler loomed large in his imagination.

Still, there's not a lot of evidence that Lee's tales were much influenced by his Jewish heritage, or that he drew on that heritage in creating his characters and plots. True, his family attended synagogue, and he had a bar mitzvah ceremony. But every religious tradition offers large and enduring themes, involving moral awakening, personal responsibility, the good and evil inside all of us, temptation, and redemption. Lee was able to tap into those themes, which helps give his characters their lasting appeal.

In that respect, Lee had a great deal in common with George Lucas, who was also able to offer variations on universals. As we have seen, Lucas was greatly influenced by Joseph Campbell and his book, *The Hero with a Thousand Faces*, which argued that many heroes, in many myths and religions, followed a similar arc ("the monomyth").[27] Recall that the arc had many ingredients, but as Campbell summarized it: "A hero ventures forth from the world of common day into a region of supernatural wonder: fabulous forces are there encountered and a decisive victory is won: the hero comes back from this mysterious adventure with the power to bestow boons on his fellow man."[28]

As far as I am aware, there is no evidence that Lee read Campbell, but the lives of many of Marvel's superheroes included important features of the monomyth, providing them enduring and cross-cultural appeal, and evidently tapping into something in the human spirit. It helped, of course, that Lee was also a terrific, inventive storyteller, with a pathbreaking insistence on seeing vulnerability, neediness, and sweetness in superheroes (Spider-Man was just a teenager who felt shy and awkward around girls).

The Jackpot

But one more time: that wasn't Lee's secret sauce. It was his exuberance—contagious, joyful, defiant, and impossible to resist. When Peter Parker first meets the gorgeous Mary Jane Watson, the love of his life, her first words to him are these: "Face it, tiger . . . You just hit the jackpot!" For decades, one of Lee's favorite words was "Excelsior!" In 2010, he offered a definition (on Twitter no less): "Upward and onward to greater glory!"[29]

These are, of course, points about Lee, and about what made him unique as a writer. But crucially, he also turned out to be an astonishing marketeer and messenger. He gave his readers a sense, in those heady days in the 1960s, that they were part of a club, one of rebels and insiders, filled with inside jokes and winks. In Lee's telling, his readers were insurgents, cooler than the rest, in on a secret. They were all Holden Caulfield (from J. D. Salinger's triumph, *The Catcher in the Rye*).

Lee published letters from readers in his comic books; they too were funny and exuberant, and they celebrated Marvel. Lee added columns, called "Bullpen Bulletins" and "Stan's Soapbox." They pulled back the curtain on the work of the writers and artists; they sought to create a network. A glimpse:

> For those of you who keep track of such minutae [sic], it's been about ten years since the Marvel Age of Comics first exploded upon the literary scene. . . . We're now faced with the task of proving that our past success wasn't merely a flash-in-the-pan; of proving that we can once again rekindle the excitement, the wonder, and the dazzling dynamism that have made Marvel a household word wherever magazines are read.[30]

The ending is characteristic Stan Lee, with the alliterative "dazzling dynamism" and the over-the-top, tongue-in-cheek, but also hoping-to-make-it-so suggestion that Marvel has become a household word.

Lee created a group of insiders, and he also created a group of outsiders. He referred to DC as "Branch-Echh" (a parody of Brand X, the term that advertisers used to refer to a competing product). He told readers about his own stable of writers and artists, and he gave them nicknames. Jack Kirby was Jack "King" Kirby; Steve Ditko was "Smilin'" Steve Ditko. As Lee put it, "I put everybody's name, I even put the letterer's name down. . . . I wanted the readers to get to know who we were and to become fans. I wanted to personalize things."

Lee sought "to give it a friendly feeling, as though we're all part of one group and we enjoy what we're doing and we know each other."[31] Readers loved that. When Marvel sold nearly eight million more magazines in 1964 than in 1960, it was clear that Lee's approach was working.[32]

We should now be able to see that Lee's success depended on a particular kind of dazzling dynamics, to wit, those traced in chapter 3. Marvel benefited, and continues to benefit, from informational cascades, which could be found for all of Lee's iconic figures, including Spider-Man, Hulk, Iron Man, Black Panther, and Thor. In the 1960s, reputational cascades were also at work: in certain circles, a ten-year-old who could not name the members of the Fantastic Four would seem impossibly out of it. I have emphasized that Marvel became a network. Perhaps above all, Lee succeeded in creating a sense of a club, which meant that group polarization would benefit Marvel. Kids created their own groups, bottom-up rather than top-down, to celebrate new issues and developments, and to ponder what would come next.

Lee's exuberance was, and is, contagious. Here's what he had to say about his team's attitude toward their work: "Many of you unsung heroes have written to ask how we really feel about our own mags. You inquired whether we take them seriously, or just treat them as a patently pointless put on." His answer: "Well, just for the record, Charlie, we BELIEVE in our swingin' superheroes!"

That they did. And for the record, Charlie, so do we.

CHAPTER 8

Bob Dylan and Habituation

Human beings habituate.[1] If you buy a new car, you will probably enjoy it a great deal in the first week, but after a while, it will just be a car. The first weeks in a new city can be entrancing, but after a certain period, things might get routine. If you move to a place with cold weather, you will notice the cold less on the fourth day than on the first, and by the end of a month, you might not notice it much at all. Bright colors tend to turn gray. Actually, that is literally true: if you stare at certain colored designs long enough and do not move your head, the colors will begin to fade.[2]

Music in particular, and art in general, are often dishabituating; they make you move your head. If they turn out to be too familiar, you will not move your head; you will see only gray. The work of the most successful musicians and artists is unfamiliar enough to be interesting, but also familiar enough to be comprehensible and to produce a kind of click of recognition. Are the greatest innovators also plagiarists? You bet.

We do have to be careful here. Some music, and some art, are not dishabituating at all. They are familiar. For that reason, they might be comforting, and comfort can sell. At one point, the Rolling Stones were dishabituating (listen to "Get Off of My Cloud"), but for decades, they have played what audiences seem to want: their well-known hits from long ago. The design of the MacBook Air was often described as iconic, and that iconic design stayed the same for many years. Still, the most successful and enduring work, in the arts and in business, delivers an initial jolt.

A great deal of research on well-being emphasizes two values: pleasure and purpose.[3] A day is filled with pleasure if it involves fun and happy experiences—television shows that you adore, a thrilling movie, terrific meals. Some companies make a lot of money because they offer a promise of days like that. A day is filled with purpose if it involves meaningful experiences—productive work, helping others, caring for your parents or your children, a sense of accomplishment or achievement. Some companies make a lot of money because they promise to provide a sense of purpose, perhaps for their employees, perhaps for their customers. But psychological research has also emphasized something different from pleasure and purpose: a "psychologically rich life," which involves variety and diversity of experiences.[4]

A psychologically rich life, with a wide range of experiences, may or may not be pleasurable or a ton of fun. We can easily imagine a psychologically rich month that sacrifices pleasure for the sake of psychological richness. You might have a vacation in a place that is interesting, even fascinating, but that has horrible food, harrowing traffic, and uncomfortable beds. It might not be a happy time. But you might be glad or even thrilled, at least in retrospect, that you endured it.

Many people who have had military experiences cherish them because they added both meaning and psychological richness. But a psychologically rich life, with a wide range of experiences, may or may not be full of a sense of meaning. At the very least, you could imagine a psychologically rich month that sacrifices purpose or meaning for the sake of its richness. You might spend a week on a gorgeous beach, with incredible sights and sounds. The week might not be very meaningful, but it might add a lot to your life. Many people value psychological richness as such, and would be willing to sacrifice pleasure and purpose for the sake of it.[5]

One reason may well be that people habituate to both pleasure and purpose. By definition, they will not habituate to the diversity and variety that constitute psychological richness.

The Mad Ones

In 1957, Jack Kerouac wrote a sentence that, for a time, was placed on posters in high schools and colleges all across the United States: "The only people for me are the mad ones, the ones who are mad to live, mad to talk, mad to be saved, desirous of everything at the same time, the ones who never yawn or say a commonplace thing, but burn, burn, burn like fabulous yellow roman candles exploding like spiders across the stars . . ."[6] That sentence benefited from an informational cascade. Over forty years later, Bob Dylan quoted the passage nearly verbatim in an interview, when speaking of his time in Greenwich Village:

I fell into that atmosphere of everything Kerouac was saying about the world being completely mad, and the only people for him that were interesting were the mad people, "the mad ones, the ones who [were] mad to live, mad to talk, mad to be saved, desirous of everything at the same time, the ones who never yawn," all of those mad ones, and I felt like I fit right into that bunch.[7]

Kerouac's sentence opposes people who yawn and say common-place things to those who are "desirous of everything at the same time" and "burn burn burn."[8]

Here is something that Bob Dylan said in an interview with Nat Hentoff:

Folk music is a bunch of fat people. I have to think of all this as traditional music. Traditional music is based on hexagrams. It comes about from legends, Bibles, plagues, and it revolves around vegetables and death. There's nobody that's going to kill traditional music. All these songs about roses growing out of people's brains and lovers who are really geese and swans that turn into angels—they're not going to die. It's all those paranoid people who think that someone's going to come and take away their toilet paper—*they're* going to die. Songs like "Which Side Are You On?" and "I Love You, Porgy"—they're not folk-music songs; they're political songs. They're *already* dead.[9]

Note the operative distinction here. On the one hand, we find "songs about roses growing out of people's brains and lovers who are really geese." Those songs are traditional. They revolve around "vegetables and death" (and so they are alive). On the other hand, we find "a bunch of fat people" and "political songs." Traditional music is immortal. Political songs are written by people who are afraid that someone is going to take away their toilet paper. (Pause over that.) They're already dead. Dylan said, "Museums are vulgar. They're all against sex."[10]

Why did Dylan succeed? We can offer a narrative, but we know enough to know that there are no simple answers to that question. Leo Tolstoy began *Anna Karenina* with this famous sentence: "Happy families are all alike; every unhappy family is unhappy in its own way." That is wrong, of course. Happy families are not alike; each is happy in its own way. Every successful artist succeeds in their own way, and something analogous is true of every failed artist.

Still, network effects played a massive role in Dylan's success, and so did group polarization. In April 2023, I spoke at the World of Bob Dylan conference at the University of Tulsa, sponsored by the University's Institute for Bob Dylan Studies. Hundreds of people were there. All of them were Dylan specialists. It seemed like a kind of pilgrimage. When I gave my speech, I was astonished to see that everyone in the audience seemed to get every Dylan reference, however obscure.

To my amazement, a friend of mine from Washington, DC—a law professor working in a high position in the Department of Justice—came up to me in the halls. I wondered: "Are you speaking too?" He responded: "No, not at all, I just wanted to be here."

"To Join Little Richard"

Born and raised in Hibbing, Minnesota, Robert Zimmerman started, in high school, as a rock and roll enthusiast. His yearbook goal: "to join Little Richard."[11]

Could Robert Zimmerman have become a rock and roll star, a bit like Elvis Presley? He certainly did not have a promising name.

That could be changed, and it was. But did he have the talent, the style, or the look? Maybe the talent, but probably not the style or the look, at least not in the early days. In the summer of 1959, he played piano, briefly, with moderately successful rock groups in Fargo, North Dakota, but they dropped him.[12] He returned to Hibbing and in the fall, Zimmerman enrolled at the University of Minnesota. There Zimmerman discovered Dinkytown, a small business district featuring used bookstores and bars—and folk music.[13]

Zimmerman more or less fell in love. Folk music appealed to something deep within him. As he put it: "There were great catch-phrases and driving pulse rhythms [in rock], but the songs weren't serious or didn't reflect life in a realistic way. I knew that when

Young Bob Dylan with Joan Baez

Source: Rowland Scherman, *Civil Rights March on Washington, D.C. [Entertainment: closeup view of vocalists Joan Baez and Bob Dylan.],* August 28, 1963.

I got into folk music, it was more of a serious type of thing. The songs are filled with more despair, more sadness, more triumph, more faith in the supernatural, and much deeper feelings."[14] (Was his shift to folk music also a career move? Possibly. Later he insisted that it was.)

Zimmerman traded in his electric guitar for an acoustic one. He changed his name—first to Robert Allyn, then to Bob Dylan.[15] Why? No one really knows. Did he want not to seem Jewish? He has given many explanations. Here's a dodge, and a good one: "Some people—you're born, you know, the wrong names, wrong parents. I mean, that happens. You call yourself what you want to call yourself. This is the land of the free."[16] The sentiment here is pretty close to that in a passage in *Chronicles,* volume 1, speaking of reading Rimbaud: "I came across one of his letters called 'Je est un autre,' which translates into 'I is someone else.' When I read those words the bells went off. It made perfect sense. I wished someone would have mentioned that to me earlier."[17]

Here's a more specific explanation of why he changed his name:

I mean, it wouldn't've worked if I'd changed the name to Bob Levy. Or Bob Neuwirth. Or Bob Doughnut. A lot of people are under the impression that Jews are just money lenders and merchants. A lot of people think that all Jews are like that. Well, they used to because that's all that was open to them. That's all they were allowed to do.[18]

Let's pause over that. Dylan thought that he could not have succeeded if he had kept a Jewish name. A singer-songwriter named Bob Dylan was not, of course, destined for success. But a singer-songwriter named Bob Zimmerman was destined for failure. Ironically, one of Dylan's heroes was a terrific folksinger named

Ramblin' Jack Elliott. (Listen to his version of "If I Were a Carpenter," which is the best there is.) Ramblin' Jack looked and dressed like a cowboy. Was he from Texas? Oklahoma? Actually, he was born in Brooklyn, and his name was Elliott Charles Adnopoz. His father, Abraham Adnopoz, was a doctor. Growing up, Elliott did not do a lot of ramblin'.

Entranced by folk music, Dylan played in the Dinkytown coffeehouses and got pretty good—not very good, but pretty good. In January 1961, he moved to New York, in part to visit the great Woody Guthrie, whom he did indeed visit and to some extent befriend.[19] Guthrie liked Dylan: "Pete Seeger's a singer of folksongs, not a folksinger. Bobby Dylan is a folksinger."[20]

In Greenwich Village, Dylan encountered and learned from the local masters, including Dave Van Ronk, known as the Mayor of MacDougal Street.[21] After a period of mimicking Guthrie on stage at small clubs in Greenwich Village (Café Wha, the Gaslight, Gerde's Folk City), he became a folksinger in his own right, writing his own songs.

That was an innovation, and its importance cannot be overstated. In the world of folk music at the time, it was considered inappropriate and even blasphemous to write new songs. The whole point of folk music was to sing old songs—the songs of the folk. (Connie Converse wrote her own songs, too, and did that before Dylan, but as we have seen, no one knew that.)

But Dylan thought he had something to say. And many decades later, Dylan connected the old and the new: "These songs didn't come out of thin air. I didn't just make them up out of whole cloth. . . . It all came out of traditional music," including traditional folk music. He added, "If you sang 'John Henry' as many times as me . . . you'd have written 'How many roads must a man walk down?' too."[22]

In the early 1960s, the local masters of folk music there in the Village did not make albums, nominally because albums seemed commercial and impure, perhaps because they did not have the opportunity. Somehow Dylan got a chance, and he did not pass it up. On September 14, 1961, Dylan happened to meet John Hammond, the legendary talent scout at Columbia Records.[23] Born in 1910, Hammond had helped to discover or promote Benny Goodman, Billie Holiday, Count Basie, Pete Seeger, and many others.[24] It is worth asking: Without John Hammond, what would have happened to Dylan?

Hammond first heard the unknown Dylan when he was playing harmonica at a session at the apartment of Carolyn Hester, a prominent folksinger.[25] Hammond reported that he decided to sign Dylan on the spot. Whether or not that was so, Dylan's recording sessions did not go easily. According to Hammond, "Bobby popped every *p*, hissed every *s*, and habitually wandered off mike. . . . Even more frustrating, he refused to learn from his mistakes. It occurred to me at the time that I'd never worked with anyone so undisciplined before."[26] The resulting album, called *Bob Dylan*, was released in 1962. It contained only two original songs. It received little critical attention and sold poorly. At Columbia, it was widely known as "Hammond's folly."[27]

In view of that unpromising debut, executives at the company suggested that Dylan should be dropped, but Hammond vigorously defended him.[28] From April 1962 to April 1963, Dylan recorded a new album, a radical departure from his first release, and it might still be his best. (This is despite its excruciating name, inspired perhaps by Ramblin' Jack Elliott: *The Freewheelin' Bob Dylan*.) At the time, Dylan happened to be dating Suze Rotolo, who was politically engaged.[29] Under her influence, Dylan produced a number of songs with strong political overtones: "Masters of War," "A Hard

Rain's A-Gonna Fall," "Oxford Town," and "Talkin' World War III Blues." Astonishingly, the outtakes from that album, released in 1991 and also with political overtones, can stand with the best songs on it: "Let Me Die in My Footsteps," "Hero Blues," "Ballad of Hollis Brown," "The Death of Emmett Till," and "Walls of Red Wing."

Between 1963 and 1965, Dylan wrote a startling number of now-classic folk songs, including "All I Really Want to Do," "It Ain't Me Babe," "Chimes of Freedom," "Mr. Tambourine Man," "It's All Over Now, Baby Blue," and "The Times They Are A-Changin'." (Were these really folk songs? A fair question.) To his great dismay, Dylan was labeled a "protest singer" and seen as "the voice of his generation." A press conference in 1965 featured this exchange:[30]

> *Interviewer:* Of the people who labour in the same musical field as you do, how many are protest singers, that is people who use the songs to protest the social state in which we live? Are there that many?
>
> *Dylan:* Yeah, you could say, 136.
>
> *Interviewer:* You mean exactly 136?
>
> *Dylan:* Ah, well, it might be 132.

Asked what "the word protest mean[s]," he answered, "singing against your wishes." He added, "I sing love songs."[31]

In March 1965, "Dylan went electric."[32] At the height of his popularity, he switched course. To the dismay of countless fans, who felt betrayed, Dylan abandoned folk music. He hired a loud, terrific band, featuring the legendary Mike Bloomfield on lead guitar.[33] He sang rock and roll. He was famously booed at the Newport Folk Festival, where he had been a hero, a kind of god.[34] He wrote "Like a Rolling Stone," maybe the greatest popular song ever. He wrote "Desolation Row," "Tombstone Blues," "Ballad of a Thin Man," "Highway 61 Revisited," "Visions of Johanna," and "I Want You." In June 1966, he was in a motorcycle accident, with injuries of unclear severity; exhausted and miserable, he took several years off from touring.[35]

Dylan returned in 1967 and 1969 with something altogether new and different—not rock and roll, closer to folk music, but with a strong country flavor. *Nashville Skyline*, released in 1969, sounded like country music. In 1975, he produced *Blood on the Tracks*, which many regard as his masterpiece. Pause over the title, if you would; it is a terrific pun. The album grows out of the collapse of Dylan's marriage, and there is a lot of blood on those tracks. The album is also a return to rock and roll, or something like it. Listen to "Idiot Wind," "Tangled Up in Blue," the soaring "Shelter from the Storm," and the gentle, joyful "Buckets of Rain."

Not long thereafter, Dylan became a born-again Christian, or so it appeared. Between 1979 and 1983, he released four gospel albums. One was called *Saved*; another was called *Infidels*. He remained active but had no major achievements until 1989, when he made "Oh Mercy," what many felt was a return to form.

Between 1997 and 2003, he returned to rock and roll with what many people think of as his great, late-career trilogy. In 2009, Dylan produced a Christmas album, followed by three albums covering pop standards, largely from the generation that preceded him (Frank Sinatra, Dean Martin, Bing Crosby). In 2020, he released *Rough and Rowdy Ways*, which peaked at number one—in a number of nations. It featured a single, "Murder Most Foul," which became his first song to be ranked first on any Billboard chart.[36]

This is a ridiculously brisk summary of Dylan's career, and of course it is highly selective. No one should question Dylan's greatness, but consider just a few of the early events that made his success possible: failure rather than success in Fargo, proximity to Dinkytown, learning about Woody Guthrie, mentorship in Greenwich Village, encountering John Hammond, dating Suze Rotolo.

Busy Being Born

"He not busy being born is busy dying," sings Dylan in "It's Alright, Ma (I'm Only Bleeding)." Those words have been repeated so often that they have become a platitude and so a bit lifeless—but that is not Dylan's fault.

I have said that on one conception of art, including music, dishabituation is its central point. It jolts listeners, viewers, and readers out of the routine and the mundane; it shows them that what seems routine and mundane is not that at all, at least if you look at it in a certain kind of way. Consider this exchange:[37]

Interviewer: Are you in love at the moment?

Dylan: I'm *always* in love.

By its nature, being in love is a state of dishabituation. In an interview, Bob Dylan once said, "I don't consider myself happy and I don't consider myself unhappy. I've just never thought of life in terms of happiness and unhappiness. It just never occurred to me."[38] From "Maggie's Farm": "They sing while you slave and I just get bored."

Dylan was, and is, a master of dishabituation. Turn in this light to "Desolation Row," and in particular to the last stanza, which is the big reveal, the clue to all that comes before. Dylan refers to a letter he received yesterday, "about the time the doorknob broke." He adds: "When you asked how I was doing/Was that some kind of joke?" He refers to people that the same "you" mentioned, whom he sees as "quite lame," which meant that he "had to rearrange their faces/And give them all another name." He asks for "no more letters" unless they are mailed "from Desolation Row."

What is this stanza about? It is a radical departure from everything that preceded it (in a very long song). The song had been about the blind commissioner, whom they've got in a trance; Cinderella, who puts her hands in her back pockets, Bette Davis style; Romeo, who is moaning; Cain and Abel; the hunchback of Notre Dame; the Good Samaritan, who is dressing and getting ready for the show; Ophelia, already an old maid, though just twenty-two; Einstein, disguised as Robin Hood, and famous long ago for playing the electric violin; Dr. Filth and his nurse; the Phantom of the Opera; Casanova; Ezra Pound and T. S. Eliot, who are fighting in the captain's tower. (So Desolation Row turns out to be the opposite of Desolation Row. It is full of life; it is not really desolate.)

From this phantasmagoria, the song suddenly flips to the first person and the mundane (and the desolate). Has the singer lost his mind? Has he woken from a dream?

The letter, perhaps from his mother, was "about the time the doorknob broke." In the letter or on the phone, she asked how he was doing. For that question, he has no patience: "Was that some kind of joke?" (Is there anything more lifeless than the abstract question, "How are you doing?") The letter mentions those "people," perhaps family and friends, whom the singer finds "quite lame." For that reason, he had to rearrange their faces and give them new names. Did they become the very characters in the song we have just heard? Probably. In any case, the singer does not want any more letters, not unless they come from Desolation Row.

The song draws an opposition. On the one hand, we have the wildness and the vitality of those at the circus. "Desolation Row" is teeming with surprises, colors, and life. It is populated by people who come from legends, Bibles, and plagues, and it revolves around vegetables and death. On the other hand, there is the mind-numbing gray of the how-are-you-doing letter. The song lays down the law: nothing more about the time the doorknob broke.

Dylan's distanced and occasionally brutal reaction to the protest movements of the 1960s is best understood in this light. Such movements became routinized, rote, deadening, the opposite of art. In that sense, their songs are not protest songs at all (not really). In his words: "Now there's a lot of people writing songs on protest subjects. . . . But the ones I've heard—there's this very emptiness which is like a song written, 'Let's hold hands and everything will be grand.' I see no more to it than that. Just because someone mentions the word 'bomb,' I'm not going to go 'Aalee!' and start clapping."[39]

In his account, "the word 'protest' . . . was made up for people undergoing surgery. It's an amusement park word . . . . The word 'message' strikes me as having a hernia-like sound. It's just like the word 'delicious.' Also the word 'marvelous.'"[40] Here is how Dylan first introduced "Blowin' in the Wind" in 1962: "This here ain't no protest song or anything like that, 'cause I don't write no protest songs."[41]

Asked in 1965 whether "The Times They Are A-Changin'" was about generational conflict, he said, "That's not what I was saying. It happened maybe that those were the only words I could find to separate aliveness from deadness. It has nothing to do with age."[42]

The philosophy of modern song, as he sees it, is his play on Keats: "Truth is chaos. Maybe beauty is chaos."[43] (That is much better than Keats' "beauty is truth, truth beauty," because it is less predictable and less sanctimonious. It is also truer.) This is also the philosophy of modern song, according to Dylan: "Greed and lust I can understand, but I can't understand the values of definition and confinement. Definition destroys."[44] In 1984, Dylan said this: "If I didn't have anything different to say to people, then what would be the point of it? I mean . . . I could do a Ronettes album!"[45]

Younger Now

Consider in this regard the famous lines from "My Back Pages": "Ah, but I was so much older then/I'm younger than that now." That declaration of youth is offered in a particular context, which is a lament about the homilies to which his younger/older self subscribed. For example: "Equality I spoke the word/As if a wedding vow." A wedding vow is, of course, a statement of commitment. (And who wants to marry a political ideal?) The song looks back on that statement—and also the cry, "Rip down all hate"—as desiccated and dead. In an (infamous) extemporaneous speech in 1963, Dylan said, "It's took me a long time to get young, and now I consider myself young. And I'm proud of it. I'm proud that I'm young."[46]

When asked why he switched to electronic music, Dylan reported:

I was doing fine, you know, singing and playing my guitar. It was a sure thing, don't you understand, it was a sure thing. I was getting very bored with that. I couldn't go out and play like that. I was thinking of quitting. Out front it was a sure thing. I knew what the audience was gonna do, how they would react. It was very automatic. Your mind just drifts unless you can find some way to get in there and remain totally there.[47]

That is an unambiguous description of habituation—of a deadened world, in which everything is predictable and automatic, so much so that one is barely even there. Dylan's antipathy to what is "already dead" helps account for his many shifts—from folksinger to rock musician, from rock musician to country musician, from country musician to gospel singer and religious zealot, from gospel singer and religious zealot to singer of traditional songs (among other things). Asked whether Woody Guthrie's songs got to him, he said, "Oh yeah. Because they were original, they just had a mark of originality on them, well the lyrics did."[48] Dylan was influenced by John Jacob Niles, about whom he had this to say: "A Mephisthophelean character out of Carolina, he hammered away at some harp-like instrument and sang in a bone chilling soprano voice. Niles was eerie and illogical, terrifically intense and gave you goose-bumps."[49]

In "All I Really Want to Do," the singer addresses a lover or an audience, or both:

I ain't lookin' to block you up
Shock or knock or lock you up
Analyze you, categorize you
Finalize you or advertise you

The song is not only about the singer's address to another; it is also what the singer expects or hopes from others. Friendship does not involve analysis or categorization, much less finalization or

advertising. The same sentiment comes through in a more romantic (and much sexier) form in "Isis":

> She said, "Where ya been?" I said, "No place special"
> She said, "You look different." I said, "Well, I guess"
> She said, "You been gone." I said, "That's only natural"
> She said, "You gonna stay?" I said, "If you want me to, yes"

Dylan famously had this to say about "Like a Rolling Stone": "I
found myself writing this story, this long piece of vomit, twenty
pages long. It was just a rhythm thing on a paper, all my steady
hatred directed at some point that was honest . . . out of it I took
'Like a Rolling Stone.'"[50] If you read the words of the song on the
page, you can understand its origins in "steady hatred":

> Now you don't talk so loud
> Now you don't seem so proud
> About having to be scrounging your next meal

That is harsh. But if you listen to those words as Dylan sings
them, you immediately see that the song is not great because it dis-
plays pleasure or glee in the downfall of someone who once rode
high. That would be cheap and lifeless. ("Positively 4th Street"
goes there, and although it is terrific in its way, it is also, for Dylan,
a bit cheap and lifeless.) What makes "Like a Rolling Stone" great,
a new national anthem, is that it is a song of chainlessness, also
known as freedom:

> How does it feel, ah how does it feel?
> To be on your own, with no direction home
> Like a complete unknown, like a rolling stone

Of course these words can be, and have been, sung in many different ways. But as Dylan sings them, the steady hatred, directed at some place that is honest, is not exactly not there, but it is transformed into a celebration ("ah how does it feel"), coming from some place that is honest—an exhilarating celebration of chaos, legends, unpredictability, change, the mad ones, plagues, and being busy being born.

Asked whether he thinks of life "in terms of growth," Dylan responded: "No! I never think in terms of growth. I tell what I do think though, that you never stop anywhere, there's no place to stop in. You know them places at the side of the road that you can stop, they're just an illusion."[51] Asked whether he sees himself "just moving onward," Dylan answered: "I see everybody like that, I see the whole world that way. That which doesn't do that is stuff that's . . . that's just dead."[52]

Speaking of the Western canon, Harold Bloom wrote that "the desire to write greatly is the desire to be elsewhere, in a time and place of one's own, in an originality that must compound with inheritance, with the anxiety of influence."[53] That captures something essential about Bob Dylan.

Let's return to "Isis," Dylan's ode to dishabituation. The first lines are clearly about moving onward:

I married Isis on the fifth day of May
But I could not hold on to her very long.
So I cut off my hair and I rode straight away
For the wild unknown country where I could not go wrong

Here once more are the most romantic lines Dylan ever wrote, with the final word of the stanza recalling the end of Joyce's *Ulysses* (but now spoken by a man, not Molly Bloom):

She said, "Where ya been?"
I said, "No place special"
She said, "You look different."
I said, "Well, I guess"
She said, "You been gone."
I said, "That's only natural"
She said, "You gonna stay?"
I said, "If you want me to, yes"

And then the end of the song, the key to everything that came before:

I still can remember the way that you smiled
On the fifth day of May in the drizzlin' rain

CHAPTER 9

Houdini's Greatest Challenge

W hat is the greatest competition in American history?
In boxing, you might single out Muhammad Ali
against Joe Frazier, or perhaps Jack Dempsey against
Gene Tunney. In chess, it has to be Bobby Fischer against Boris
Spassky. In politics, it might be John F. Kennedy against Richard
Nixon, or perhaps Abraham Lincoln against Stephen Douglas.
But in terms of sheer human drama, there is a strong argument
that all of these were topped by the pitched battle, both personal
and intellectual, between Harry Houdini, the great debunker of
self-proclaimed psychics, and Mina Crandon, the most compelling
psychic of the twentieth century. Both of them were ridiculously
famous—Houdini because he was, well, Houdini, and Crandon
because she seemed to have supernatural powers. Featured repeatedly in the nation's leading newspapers, Crandon was Houdini's
hardest case and his greatest nemesis. By the way, the two might
have been in love with each other.

In the 1920s, some of the world's greatest thinkers were convinced that people could speak to the dead. Sir Arthur Conan

Doyle created Sherlock Holmes, the canonical detective, who could always see through fakery and artifice. But having lost a son in the Great War, Doyle was also a "convinced Spiritualist" who thought death "rather an unnecessary thing."[1] In his popular 1918 book, *The New Revelation*, he argued vigorously on behalf of Spiritualism. His dedication: "To all the brave men and women, humble or learned, who have the moral courage during seventy years to face ridicule or worldly disadvantage in order to testify to an all-important truth."[2] From 1919 to 1930, Doyle wrote fifteen more books on the same subject.[3]

One of Doyle's allies was the eminent British physicist Sir Oliver Lodge, who had done important work on the discharge of electricity, X-rays, and radio signals.[4] Lodge contended that he was in touch with Raymond, his dead son; he wrote a book about their communication and the science that explained it.[5] President of the British Society for Psychical Research (originally led by Cambridge's Henry Sidgwick, probably the greatest philosopher of the time), Lodge sought to make a serious study of the subject.[6] Charles Richet, a professor at the College de France who had won the Nobel Prize in physiology, coined the term "ectoplasm" for the matter from which ghostly apparitions formed.[7] Thomas Edison was no Spiritualist, but he announced his intention to work on a mechanism to communicate with people who had crossed over.[8]

The era's most influential skeptic? Harry Houdini. Born Ehrich Weiss, Houdini became famous as an escape artist, but he began his career as a magician and a medium.[9] To make a living in hard times, he worked as "the celebrated Psychometric Clairvoyant," with the power to communicate with "the other side."[10] While he proved a pretty convincing psychic, he discovered that he had a unique talent, even a kind of genius: escaping the apparently inescapable. As David Jaher writes:

They locked him in a dreaded Siberian prison van, bottled him in a milk can, and entombed him in a block of ice in Holland. They shackled him to a spinning windmill, the chassis of an automobile, the muzzle of a loaded cannon. They put him in a padlocked US mailbag, roped him to the twentieth-story girder of an unfinished skyscraper, sealed him in a giant envelope, and boxed him in a crate nailed tight and dropped in New York Harbor. He emerged triumphant and smiling.[11]

Houdini's talent had a lot to do with his extraordinary physical abilities. He was strong as an ox, and he trained himself to use his toes the way most people use their fingers.[12] But he also found that he had a Sherlock Holmes–like capacity to engage in detective work. Caught in a trap, he had an ability to see, almost at a glance, the multiple steps that would enable him to find his way out.

As Houdini's fame grew, he maintained a skeptical but keen interest in spirit communication, intensified by his devastation at the death of his beloved mother (the love of his life).[13] He and Doyle were good friends, and they had many discussions of the topic, with Houdini acknowledging his desire to be convinced that Doyle was right. But everyone he encountered was a fraud, and he became the world's leading expert on the tricks, debunking some of the hardest cases. Edison himself, for example, believed that one famous "mentalist," named Bert Reiss, was in fact clairvoyant. Houdini easily demonstrated that he was a fake.[14] Because of the evident drama of the confrontation between Houdini and the self-styled mentalists (read: clever frauds), the public was intrigued.

In the 1920s, as now, *Scientific American* was a highly respected publication, dedicated to the dissemination of research findings. In 1922, Doyle challenged the magazine and its editor in chief, Orson Munn, to undertake a serious investigation of psychic

Harry Houdini

Source: Campbell-Gray, Ltd., *Harry Handcuff Houdini*, 1913.

phenomena.[15] James Malcolm Bird, an editor there (and previously a mathematics professor at Columbia University), was intrigued.[16] In November, the magazine established a highly publicized contest, with a prize of $5,000 for anyone who could produce conclusive evidence of "physical manifestations"—as, for example, by making objects fly around the room. The magazine soberly announced that as of yet, it was "unable to reach a definite conclusion as to the validity of psychic claims."[17] The competition was bound to be a public sensation, in part because of the reach of *Scientific American*, in part because of the nature of the subject matter. Were some people actually psychics?

Five judges were chosen. The most eminent was William McDougall, chairman of the Harvard psychology department and president of the American Society for Psychical Research.[18] (William James had been his predecessor in both positions.) Daniel Frost Comstock, a respected physicist and engineer, had taught at the Massachusetts Institute of Technology.[19] A PhD from Yale, Walter Franklin Prince had explored a number of purportedly supernatural events; he had always been able to offer natural explanations.[20] Hereward Carrington, a prolific author and one-time magician, specialized in exposing fakes.[21] Rounding out the committee, the magazine added Houdini, author of a forthcoming book on unmasking psychics.[22] The contest captured the public's imagination. The *New York Times* called it "the Acid Test of Spiritualism."[23]

All of the initial candidates failed that test; the committee saw through them. In the meantime, a woman named Mina Crandon was garnering attention in Boston.[24] Her husband—wealthy, handsome, and significantly older—was a prominent Harvard-trained gynecologist, married twice before.[25] In the early 1920s, Dr. Crandon attended one of Sir Oliver Lodge's lectures on Spiritualism, and the two spoke at length that night. Crandon was intrigued: "I couldn't understand it. It did not fit into any pattern I had previously known about scientists."[26] He became obsessed. According to a friend, he "had taken to the psychical research movement like a Jew to Marxism."[27] (An interesting formulation.)

His wife was witty, warm, mischievous, fun-loving, and gorgeous. One friend, speaking for many, described her as a "very very
beautiful girl" and "probably the most utterly charming woman I
have ever known."[28] Mrs. Crandon disparaged her husband's interest in Spiritualism, joking that as a gynecologist, "naturally he was
interested in exploring the netherworld."[29] Nonetheless, she thought
that "a séance sounded like great fun," and so she chose, on a kind
of lark, to attend one.[30] The medium, a local minister, claimed to
contact the spirit of Mina's brother, Walter, who had died in a tragic
accident at the age of twenty-eight.[31] The minister also told her that
"she had rare powers and soon all would know it."[32]

Not long thereafter, the Crandons hosted an unusual party at
their home on Lime Street in Boston. The purpose of the party? To
find a ghost. Mrs. Crandon found it all absurd: "They were all so
solemn about it that I couldn't help laughing."[33] But as the participants linked hands in a circle on a table, it started to vibrate, eventually crashing to the floor.[34] To see which member of the circle was
a medium, each took turns leaving the room. When Mrs. Crandon
departed, the vibrations stopped; her friends applauded when she
reentered.[35]

With the same group and a few others, the Crandons continued their experiments. Everyone who was there attested to some
remarkable events, including rapping noises and movements of the
table.[36] Six days later, Mrs. Crandon appeared to be possessed by
the spirit of her brother, who spoke in a guttural voice that could
not be recognized as her own, and who was funny and immensely
lively (and engagingly coarse and profane).[37]

Her fame began to spread in Boston. As it did, members of
the Harvard community tried to debunk her. An acquaintance of
Dr. Crandon, a psychologist named Dr. Roback, suspected "spirit
humbug," but could find no explanation for what he observed.[38] He

Mina Crandon/Margery

Source: Stanley De Brath, *Mina Crandon materialized hand*, 1930.

enlisted McDougall to help solve the mystery. Attending Mina's séances, both psychologists were baffled. Another visitor at the time said that he "was present many times when Walter's voice was as clear as that of any person in the circle," and also "close to my ear, whispering some very personal comment about me or my family."[39]

In December, Crandon and his wife traveled to Paris and London to demonstrate her abilities. She was a sensation. In London, she performed in front of several investigators, appearing to make a table rise and float.[40] The Crandons became friendly with Doyle, who swore to the truth and range of her powers. Lodge told colleagues that when they visited the United States, there were just two things that they must see: Niagara Falls and Mrs. Crandon.[41]

Intrigued by the publicity, Bird decided to visit the Crandons in Boston. He was immediately struck by her apparent sincerity, her elegance, and her keen sense of humor, which he described as "wicked."[42] It seems fair to say that he was enthralled by her. He was also amazed by what he saw in the séances, which included flashes of light, raps, whistles, and cool breezes.[43] He told Orson Munn that "there had been a war between the Crandons and the Harvard scientists." Munn asked: Who won? The medium won, Bird answered. He invited her to enter the magazine's contest.[44]

Accepting the challenge, she performed repeatedly in front of Bird and various committee members, moving objects, producing noises in various places, and channeling Walter. In the spring and summer of 1924, Bird himself visited Lime Street nearly sixty times.[45] He was convinced that Mrs. Crandon was genuine. Comstock, who attended fifty-six séances, could find nothing amiss.[46] McDougall tried for months to discover fraud, and he repeatedly accused her of fakery. But he lacked any evidence of tricks, and "she responded to his incredulity with wit."[47] Carrington initially found the reports far-fetched, but after over forty visits, he could not explain what he saw.[48]

It looked as if McDougall, Comstock, and Carrington would endorse her. Though skeptical by nature, Prince also seemed moved.[49] In the July 1924 issue of *Scientific American*, Bird wrote about her, protecting her privacy with the name "Margery." He said that "the initial probability of genuineness [is] much greater than in any previous case which the Committee has handled."[50] Bird's article was widely discussed. The topic was irresistible. A headline in the *New York Times* read, "Margery Passes All Psychic Tests."[51] The *Boston Herald* exclaimed, "Four of Five Men Chosen to Bestow Award Sure She Is 100 P.C. Genuine."[52]

Reading all this, Houdini, who had not had an opportunity to see the famous Margery in action, exploded. Traveling immediately to New York, he asked Bird if she was going to receive the prize. Bird replied, "Most decidedly."[53] Houdini insisted that it would be unfair to give her the award unless he had had his own opportunity to investigate her claims. Bird agreed, and Dr. Crandon was not pleased. Writing to Doyle before the meeting, he said, "My deep regret is that this low-minded Jew has any claim on the word American"; he described the coming encounter as "war to the finish."[54]

Mrs. Crandon's reaction was far more positive. Houdini had been a star since she was a child, and she was proud to receive him. She found him polite, curious, dignified, even enchanting. On the night of his arrival, she put on one of her standard performances, apparently impressing everyone with a moving cabinet, a slowed and stopped Victrola, and a bell box, which seemed to ring of its own accord.[55] As Bird drove Munn and Houdini back to their hotel, Munn asked Houdini what he thought. He replied immediately: "All fraud—every bit of it."[56]

Notwithstanding that judgment, he and Mrs. Crandon remained on excellent terms. He appeared to be charmed by her, and in his diary that night, he noted her beauty. A photograph was taken the next day, which Mrs. Crandon had asked Houdini to keep private. Houdini was generally formal with women, but in this picture, he is leaning very close. He "holds her hand and smiles at her affectionately—while she turns to him as if expecting a kiss."[57] In the aftermath of his visit, they enjoyed a warm correspondence. "I am glad to be able to say I know 'The Great Houdini,'" she wrote him.[58]

Observing her closely on several occasions, Houdini began to figure out exactly how she produced her effects. With evident admiration, he reported, Mrs. Crandon had produced "the 'slickest' ruse I have ever detected, and it has converted all skeptics."[59] He added, "It has taken my thirty years of experience to detect her in her various moves."[60]

In November, he wrote a lengthy pamphlet, complete with drawings of the séances, specifying exactly how Mrs. Crandon was able, in the dark, to maneuver her feet, arms, shoulders, and head to produce the various effects. "As she is unusually strong and has an athletic body," he wrote, "she can press her wrists so firmly on the arms of the chair that she can move her body and sway it at will."[61] He concluded that Mrs. Crandon is "a shrewd, cunning woman, resourceful in the extreme."[62]

Mrs. Crandon's numerous defenders were unconvinced. They portrayed Houdini as implacably closed-minded, himself a cheat. Doyle denounced Houdini as prejudiced and dishonest; the denunciation destroyed their friendship. From *Scientific American*, the official verdict came on February 12, 1925: Houdini was correct. Prince and McDougall captured the consensus with these words: "We have observed no phenomena of which we can assert that they could not have been produced by normal means."[63] The sole dissenter, Carrington, stated that he had been "convinced that genuine phenomena have occurred here."[64]

For Margery, however, that was hardly the end. Bird promptly rose to her defense, describing Houdini as a liar and an ignoramus.[65] She continued to hold séances, joking that 150 years before, she would have been executed as a witch, but "now they send committees of professors from Harvard to study me. That represents some progress, doesn't it?"[66] Even Houdini was unable to explain some of her new feats, conceding, "The lady is subtle."[67] *Life* magazine said that she was "almost as hard to bury as the League of Nations."[68]

But as the months and years went by, her act seemed decreasingly credible. A new group of Harvard researchers undertook a six-month investigation and found strong evidence of trickery.[69] In 1930, the ever-loyal Bird, who worked to discredit the Harvard study, confessed that to fool Houdini, Margery had solicited his help in producing some of her effects. While continuing to believe that she was genuine, Bird acknowledged that when put "in a situation where she thought she might have to choose between fraud and a blank séance," she "chose fraud."[70] Most damningly, researchers exposed one of her most bizarre effects, in which "Walter" seemed to make his own fingerprint appear on wax. The print turned out to be identical to that of Mrs. Crandon's dentist.[71]

As it happens, a lot was going on at 10 Lime Street in the mid-1920s. Late in her life, Mrs. Crandon spoke fondly of her affair with Carrington, her only loyalist on the committee.[72] (Perhaps he enjoyed attesting that "genuine phenomena have occurred here.") Bird also claimed to have had a romance, though that might have been his imagination; she described him as "disgusting."[73] Both McDougall and Prince reported that she attempted to seduce them.[74]

Houdini said something similar, adding, "When I walked into the séance room and saw that beautiful blonde, her applesauce meant nothing to me. I have been through apple orchards."[75] But all the while, she spoke well of him: "I respect Houdini more than any of the bunch. He has both feet on the ground all the time."[76] And she expressed genuine sorrow at his death, singling out his virility, his determination, and his courage.

At a certain level of abstraction, Mrs. Crandon's fame is not so difficult to explain. At the time, respected thinkers were intrigued by the idea of psychic phenomena and of contact with the dead. Part of that was genuine uncertainty. Part of it was wishful thinking. Mrs. Crandon was extremely clever, and she was able to fool people who were trained to detect fraud. It did not hurt that she was beautiful and charming. In the circumstances, an informational cascade in her favor is not at all surprising. And the little group that was supposed to assess her veracity seemed to be a victim of group polarization—until Houdini entered the scene and ruined everything.

A psychological mystery remains: What led Mrs. Crandon to do what she did? Here's a guess. By 1923, her marriage was troubled. Dr. Crandon was depressive, intensely hardworking, and obsessed by Spiritualism. Playful, resourceful, and competitive, his wife was initially willing to have some fun with the topic. But as she learned, she was also exceptionally talented, a natural magician— and her talent operated in precisely the domain that most interested her husband. As she became well-known, things started to get out of hand. What started as a kind of game, essentially with friends, turned into international news. And when that happened, she enlisted her husband, Carrington, Bird, and undoubtedly others as accomplices. Importantly, her role as Margery also created a kind of marital glue. She was stuck in it.

Why did so many people believe that Margery was not a fake? Were they irrational? Actually not. We have seen that a lot of people thought that it might be possible to contact the dead. Also they *wanted* to believe that. True, many people were skeptical, but it was enthralling to think that she might have supernatural powers. And how likely was it that a young housewife, without apparent financial motives, would have the desire, and the skills, to do what Mrs. Crandon did? To move furniture, make rapping noises, ring bells, and produce an apparently male voice, altogether different from her own? As improbable as contact with "the other side" might have seemed, the complexity, sophistication, and evident credibility of the alleged fraud might have appeared less probable still.

This little tale, largely lost to history, can easily be dismissed as a curiosity, when highly educated citizens of a barely recognizable United States, just entering modernity, were willing to believe in crazy things. But any such dismissal would be a mistake. All over the world, people continue to believe in magic, miracles, psychics, and spirits, and a lot of them are highly educated. Many people scoff at science, or at least distrust the scientific consensus. They do not believe the experts; they believe what they see, and the people they trust. They think what they like to think. They like to see magic. They are moved by their own Margerys, who may have an extraordinary talent, the defining skill of the magician, which is to put their audience's attention exactly and only where they want it. (Many of the best politicians have the same skill.) Cascades, network effects, and group polarization might result. So might fame.

Consider a little tale from one of Margery's investigators, Princeton psychologist Henry McComas, who described her supernatural feats to Houdini with great wonder, insisting that he saw every one of them with his own eyes. McComas reported that for the rest of his life, he would never forget the scorn with which Houdini greeted those words. "You say, you *saw*. Why you didn't see anything. What do you see now?"[77] At that point, Houdini slapped a half-dollar between his palms, and it promptly disappeared.

His great adversary never confessed. In her very last days, a researcher suggested to a failing Mrs. Crandon, widowed for two years, that she would die happier if she finally did so, and let the world know about her methods. To his surprise, her old twinkle of merriment returned to her eyes. She laughed softly and offered her answer: "Why don't you guess?"[78]

CHAPTER 10

The Cult of Ayn Rand

As a teenager, I fell for Ayn Rand.

More precisely, I fell for her novels. Reading *The Fountainhead* at the age of fourteen, I was overwhelmed by the passionate intensity of Rand's heroic characters. Who could forget the indomitable Howard Roark? "His face was like a law of nature—a thing one could not question, alter or implore. It had high cheekbones over gaunt, hollow cheeks; gray eyes, cold and steady; a contemptuous mouth, shut tight, the mouth of an executioner or a saint."[1] Roark was defined by his fierce independence: "I do not recognize anyone's right to one minute of my life. Nor to any part of my energy. Nor to any achievement of mine. No matter who makes the claim, how large their number or how great their need."[2]

Like countless teenage boys, I aspired to be like Roark. And I found Rand's heroine, Dominique Francon, irresistible. She was not only impossibly beautiful but brilliant, elegant, imperious, and cruel. "[S]he looked like a stylized drawing of a woman and made the correct proportions of a normal being appear heavy and awkward beside her."[3]

In Rand's operatic tales, the world is divided into two kinds of people: creators and parasites. The creator is "self-sufficient, self-motivated, self-generated."[4] His only need is independence. He lives for himself. By contrast, the parasite "lives second-hand" and depends on other people.[5] The parasite "preaches altruism"—a degrading thing—and "demands that man live for others."[6]

At first I was thrilled by Rand's narratives, in which insidious parasites tried desperately to domesticate or enfeeble the creators, who ultimately found a way to triumph by carving out their own paths. Rand seemed to reveal secrets. She seemed to offer a kind of admission ticket. She turned the world upside down. But after a few weeks of rapture, her books started to sicken me.

Contemptuous toward most of humanity, merciless about human frailty, and constantly hammering on the moral evils of redistribution, they produced a sense of claustrophobia. They had little humor or play. It wasn't that I detected a flaw in Rand's logic and decided to embrace altruism, or that I began to like the New Deal and the welfare state. It was more visceral than that. Reading and thinking about her novels was like being trapped in an elevator with someone who talked too loud, kept saying the same thing, and wouldn't shut up.

Decades later, I am struck by a puzzle. While Rand did not offer even a single interesting argument, her novels continue to resonate. Long after her death, she remains famous. Her novels have sold tens of millions of copies. Rand changes norms. She alters people's sense of what is normal and, in the process, changes lives. She speaks directly to an important part of the human soul. How does that happen?

Donald Trump, a big Rand fan, has said he identifies with Roark. *The Fountainhead*, he claims, "relates to business [and] beauty [and] life and inner emotions. That book relates to . . .

everything."[7] If we want to understand the widespread contempt for "losers," we might focus on Rand, whose "dour visage," as the cultural critic Lisa Duggan writes, "presides over the spirit of our time."[8] Rand "made acquisitive capitalism sexy. She launched thousands of teenage libidos into the world of reactionary politics on a wave of quivering excitement."[9]

Since it was published in 1943, *The Fountainhead* has sold over 9 million copies worldwide.[10] *Atlas Shrugged*, generally regarded as Rand's most influential book, has done even better, with sales in excess of 10 million.[11] She is big among successful people in business. Steve Jobs, Peter Thiel, and Jeff Bezos have all called themselves fans.[12] Prominent politicians express their admiration for her work. Former Secretary of State Mike Pompeo has said that *Atlas Shrugged* "really had an impact on me."[13] Paul Ryan, the former Speaker of the House, once professed, "The reason I got involved in public service, by and large, if I had to credit one thinker, one person, it would be Ayn Rand."[14] As her biographer Jennifer Burns puts it, "For over half a century Rand has been the ultimate gateway drug to life on the right."[15] Many people take her books, Burns goes on, as "a sort of scripture."[16] American politics and the contemporary Republican Party owe a lot to Ayn Rand.

How did this happen?

She was born Alissa Zinovievna Rosenbaum in 1905 in Saint Petersburg, to a prosperous Jewish family.[17] At thirteen she declared herself an atheist.[18] (As she later put it, she rejected the idea that God was "the greatest entity in the universe. That made man inferior and I resented the idea that man was inferior to anything."[19]) When the Bolshevik Revolution came in 1917, it hit her family hard. The pharmacy her father owned was seized and nationalized.[20] Rand's hatred of the Bolsheviks helped define her thinking about capitalism and redistribution. "I was twelve years old when I heard the slogan that man must live for the state," she later wrote, "and I thought right then that this idea was evil and the root of all the other evils we were seeing around us. I was already an individualist."[21]

The Bolshevik government shaped her future course, too, by exposing her to film. The Bolsheviks gave a great deal of support to the film industry, and Rand was enthralled by the potential of cinema and by what she was able to see of Hollywood movies.[22] In 1924 she enrolled in a state institute to learn screenwriting and decided to go to the United States in the hope of becoming a screenwriter and novelist.[23] She applied for a passport and got it. She also obtained a US visa, falsely telling a US consular official that she was engaged to a Russian man and would undoubtedly return. In 1926, she left Soviet Russia. She never saw her parents again.[24]

Not long after arriving in New York, she changed her name to Ayn Rand.[25] How did she come up with that particular name? There has been much speculation but no authoritative answer. Shades of Bob Dylan! Also note well: Alissa Zinovievna Rosenbaum might not have become a famous writer in the United States.

She soon moved to Hollywood and quickly managed to meet her favorite director, Cecil B. DeMille (it is not clear how); he hired her as a junior screenwriter.[26] She also met Frank O'Connor, a devastatingly handsome, elegant, unintellectual, mostly unsuccessful actor, of whom she said, "I took one look at him and, you know, Frank is the physical type of all my heroes. I instantly fell in love."[27] Reader, she stalked him. She and O'Connor married in 1929. They lived in California, and she continued to work as a screenwriter. From the very beginning, she was the family's breadwinner.[28]

Rand's writing career picked up a bit in the 1930s when she published her first two novels, *We the Living* and *Anthem*.[29] (Rand enthusiasts regard both as classics.) Dismayed by the policies of President Franklin Delano Roosevelt and by what she saw as collectivist tendencies in American life, she avidly read FDR haters such as Albert Jay Nock and H. L. Mencken, who called themselves "libertarians" (understood as enthusiastic advocates of free markets and skeptics about state power, ultimately giving birth to an intellectual movement that has significantly influenced American politics).[30] She began to write in defense of capitalism. In 1941, she produced a statement of principles, "The Individualist Manifesto," meant as an alternative to *The Communist Manifesto*.[31] The principles echoed through her work for the rest of her life. A sample:

> The right of liberty means man's right to individual action, individual choice, individual initiative and individual property. Without the right to private property no independent action is possible.
>
> The right to the pursuit of happiness means man's right to live for himself, to choose what constitutes his own, private, personal happiness and to work for its achievement. Each individual is the sole and final judge in this choice. A man's happiness cannot be prescribed to him by another man or by any number of other men.[32]

Written under the shadow of the manifesto and mostly in a one-year spurt of creativity, *The Fountainhead* was published in 1943.[33] It became a sensation, largely through word of mouth—an exceedingly rapid informational cascade. Readers described their reactions with words like "awakening" and "revelation."[34] Fountainheadmania was almost like a religion (and as we shall see, it eventually morphed into something very much like that). Rand became a celebrity almost overnight.

People wanted to meet her. Men in particular wanted to meet her. It is unclear whether her relationship with any of those men turned sexual, but there were serious flirtations and apparently romantic feelings.[35] Her husband's acting career was going poorly, and he was economically dependent on his wife; in many ways, their marriage represented a reversal of traditional sex roles. Rand wasn't living the man-worship depicted in her novels.

After World War II, Rand became an anti-communist Cold Warrior, testifying before the House Un-American Activities Committee about Communist infiltration of the film industry and of popular films.[36] In 1944 she started to write *Atlas Shrugged*; it took her thirteen years to finish.[37] In that period, Rand withdrew from the political fray and relied on a small social circle, a kind of group polarization machine, created for her by her most trusted acolyte, Nathan Blumenthal.[38] Blumenthal was a handsome and vibrant Canadian who had long idolized her (and who worked as a part-time psychologist using Rand's principles).[39] Twenty-five years younger than Rand, he had read and reread *The Fountainhead* at the age of fourteen, memorizing whole passages.[40] In high school and then as a student at the University of California at Los Angeles, he wrote fan letters to Rand.[41] After first ignoring them, in 1950 she invited the nineteen-year-old undergraduate to visit.[42]

Sparks flew when Blumenthal and Rand first met, at least by his account. "I felt as if ordinary reality had been left somewhere behind," he later wrote, "and I was entering the dimension of my most passionate longing."[43] They talked philosophy from 8 p.m. that night until 5:30 a.m. the next morning, while Frank sat by in silence. Blumenthal describes himself as "intoxicated"—"two souls . . . shocked by mutual recognition."[44]

A few hours after the meeting, still early in the morning, he went to the apartment of his girlfriend Barbara Weidman, also a Rand enthusiast. He was rapturous. "She's fascinating," he told Weidman. "She's Mrs. Logic."[45] A week later, Blumenthal returned to Rand's home, this time with Weidman, who reported that she "was not a conventionally attractive woman, but compelling in the remarkable combination of perceptiveness and sensuality, of intelligence and passionate intensity, that she projected."[46]

Soon Blumenthal and Rand were speaking almost every evening, sometimes for hours. The two couples—Ayn and Frank, Nathan and Barbara—become close, even intimate.[47] In 1951, Nathan and Barbara moved to New York to study at New York University.[48] Ayn and Frank joined them a few months later.[49]

These were the founding members of Rand's philosophical movement, which she called Objectivism. That movement, which continues to exist, was pivotal to Rand's lasting fame. Things definitely got weird and began to take on aspects of a personality cult. Nathan Blumenthal, with Rand's endorsement, decided to change his name to Nathaniel Branden, exclaiming, "Why should we be stuck with someone else's choice of name?"[50] In January 1953, he married Barbara Weidman, with Rand as maid of honor and Frank as best man.[51] Barbara took the invented last name, too.

In September 1954, Rand and Nathaniel declared to their spouses that they had fallen in love with each other, and Rand, the self-styled apostle of reason, calmly informed Barbara and Frank that it was only rational that they should fall in love themselves. As Rand put it, "If Nathan and I are who we are, if we see what we see in each other, if we truly hold the values we profess, how can we not be in love?"[52] But she promised that despite their feelings, the relationship between the two of them would not be physical.

"We have no future, except as friends," she told Barbara and Frank.[53] Predictably, their relationship did turn sexual.[54] But Ayn and Frank stayed married, as did Barbara and Nathaniel. Throughout the period, Rand worked intensely on *Atlas Shrugged*; Frank and both Brandens read multiple drafts.

Over a thousand pages long, the book is dystopian science fiction in which an imaginary US government has asserted almost complete regulatory control over the private sector. Its first line signals a mystery: "Who is John Galt?" Society's godlike creators (inventors, scientists, thinkers, architects, and others who do and make things), led by Galt, a Roark-like hero, decide to go on strike. They withdraw from society and watch the parasites and looters devour themselves. Ultimately their government collapses, and Galt plans to create a new society, based on principles of individualism. The final sentence of *Atlas Shrugged* captures Galt in a moment of mastery: "He raised his hand, and over the desolate earth he traced in space the sign of the dollar."

Rand dedicated her book to two people: her husband and Nathaniel Branden. Of Branden, she wrote:

When I wrote *The Fountainhead*, I was addressing myself to an ideal reader—to as rational and independent a mind as I could conceive of. I found such a reader—through a fan letter he wrote me about *The Fountainhead* when he was nineteen years old. He is my intellectual heir. His name is Nathaniel Branden.[55]

Rand predicted that *Atlas Shrugged* would "be the most controversial book of this century; I'm going to be hated, vilified, lied about, smeared in every possible way."[56] Because of the success of *The Fountainhead*, and because Rand was in a sense a cult leader by virtue of that success, *Atlas Shrugged* was bound to get a great deal of attention. This was the Matthew Effect in action. The idea that it would be "the most controversial book of this century" was characteristic Randian grandiosity—but still.

The early reviews fulfilled Rand's expectations. The most severe came from the right-of-center magazine *National Review*, where Whittaker Chambers, the ex-Communist and conservative hero, deplored her atheism and proclaimed: "Out of a lifetime of reading, I can recall no other book in which a tone of overriding arrogance is so implacably sustained. . . . From almost any page of *Atlas Shrugged*, a voice can be heard from painful necessity, commanding: 'To a gas chamber—go!'"[57]

The book became a national phenomenon, but Rand was devastated. She craved approval not from ordinary readers but from prominent thinkers, including academics, and she didn't get it. She fell into a deep depression, telling the Brandens, "John Galt wouldn't feel like this."[58] (She didn't mean this as a joke. Rand didn't do self-deprecation.) She never wrote fiction again.

Nonetheless, her influence continued to grow. Nathaniel Branden became a vigorous entrepreneur on her behalf, organizing Objectivism into various lecture series, and in 1961 creating the Nathaniel Branden Institute (NBI) in homage to her.[59] NBI was exceedingly helpful to Rand's career. It became a group polarization machine.

Four years later, the Brandens separated as a couple, but they continued to work closely together as, in Barbara's words, "comrades in arms."[60] They succeeded in producing something like an organized movement, with thirty-five hundred students in fifty cities by 1967.[61] The NBI, and Rand's social world, revolved around what she called the Collective, a small group of devotees that included Alan Greenspan, who went on to become Chairman of the Federal Reserve Board.[62] The group was unquestionably an echo chamber, dedicated to the celebration of Ayn Rand.

But something was rotten in the state of NBI. There was secrecy; the organization was led by Rand and Branden, whose passionate, turbulent relationship was known to their spouses but hidden from everyone else. There was enforced orthodoxy. Within the Collective and the NBI, Rand and Branden would not tolerate the slightest dissent. As Branden wrote in his memoir with a kind of mordant humor, students were taught the following:

- Ayn Rand is the greatest human being who has ever lived.
- *Atlas Shrugged* is the greatest human achievement in the history of the world.
- Ayn Rand, by virtue of her philosophical genius, is the supreme arbiter in any issue pertaining to what is rational, moral, or appropriate to man's life on earth.[63]

In 1968, things fell to pieces. Rand abruptly split with the Brandens, stating in a bizarre, unhinged public letter, "I hereby withdraw my endorsement of them and of their future works and activities. I repudiate both of them, totally and permanently, as spokesmen for me or for Objectivism."[64] Though she referred to various financial and personal improprieties, she did not disclose the actual reasons for the split. Both Brandens responded with public letters of their own.[65]

Neither revealed the truth, which was intensely personal. While working closely with Rand and continuing to proclaim his love for her, Nathaniel had ended their sexual relationship, citing supposed psychological problems (for which she "counseled" him).[66] All the while, he was having a secret love affair with another woman. He disclosed that relationship to Barbara as early as 1966; after repeated entreaties from Rand, asking what on earth was wrong with Nathaniel, Barbara told her the truth.[67]

Rand was shattered. Branden, she told Barbara, had taken away "this earth."[68] She fell into an implacable rage, which lasted for the rest of her life. She never spoke to Nathaniel Branden again. Barbara put it this way to Nathaniel: "Ayn wants you dead."[69] Among other things, she ordered the deletion of her glowing dedication to Nathaniel in subsequent printings of *Atlas Shrugged*.

Despite her emotional devastation, Rand continued to work and to write. She spoke on college campuses and did interviews on television, where she was often engaging, charming, and even funny. She wrote long essays for the *Objectivist* magazine and the *Ayn Rand Letter*.[70]

In the 1970s her health deteriorated. A lifelong smoker, she was diagnosed with lung cancer in 1974.[71] Five years later, Frank O'Connor died, again shattering her.[72] Rand herself died in 1982.[73] By that point, she had alienated or rejected most of her friends.

Rand has massively influenced contemporary political thought, less through her ideas than because she offered, in *The Fountainhead* and *Atlas Shrugged*, heroic accounts of capitalism and capitalists, whom she contrasted with the losers, moochers, and "second-handers" who seek to steal from them through taxes and regulation. She gave voice to, and helped spur, a specifically moral objection to redistribution of wealth and to interference with property rights and market arrangements. That objection resonates strongly in the business community and the Republican party. In a sense, Rand captures a part of the Zeitgeist; she caught a wave, and she made it bigger.

Was Rand a serious thinker? That is doubtful. She did not defend her conclusions so much as pound the table for them.

(*The Fountainhead* defined "freedom": "To ask nothing. To expect nothing. To depend on nothing."[74]) Yet she did write a great deal in an effort to justify Objectivism in strictly philosophical terms. Robert Nozick, the influential libertarian philosopher, seemed to take her seriously, and the Ayn Rand Society, affiliated with the American Philosophical Society, produces papers and books focusing on her work.[75] But anyone interested in free markets, liberty of contract, and the importance of private property would do a lot better to read Friedrich Hayek, Milton Friedman, or Nozick himself.

Rand's fame and enduring influence comes from readers' cult-like reactions to her fiction—to their response to her ability to convey the sheer exhilaration of personal defiance, human independence, and freedom from chains of all kinds. She triggered cascade effects, and she benefited from an extraordinary form of group polarization. As a result, she touched and legitimated the psychological roots of a prominent strand in right-wing thought. A skeptic about Roark's ambitious plans poses this question to him: "My dear fellow, who will let you?" Roark's answer: "That's not the point. The point is, who will stop me?"[76]

That exchange captures what many people in the United States think is not merely wrong but evil about Roosevelt's New Deal, the Affordable Care Act, the Consumer Financial Protection Bureau, the Clean Air Act, even the Civil Rights Act of 1964. Call it Who-Will-Stop-Me Capitalism. It has special resonance among adolescent boys, but its appeal is much broader than that. The problem is that those who need to lionize men with "a contemptuous mouth, shut tight, the mouth of an executioner or a saint" tend to be terrified of something.[77] Altruism really is okay. Redistribution to those who need help is not a violation of human rights.

Rand had a unique talent for transforming people's political convictions through tales of indomitable heroes and heroines, romance, and sex. Her novels have been described as "conversion machines that run on lust."[78] Decades after Rand's death, Branden seemed to agree. "[Not] just Ayn and me," he wrote, "but all of us— we were ecstasy addicts. No one ever named it that way, but that was the key."[79]

CHAPTER 11

John, Paul, George, and Ringo

When I worked for President Obama in the White House, I remember him musing: "CEOs think I hate them. I really don't. Not at all. Not in the slightest." Then he paused and said: "What I do know is that they're lucky to be where they are. They might be amazing, but still, they're lucky to be where they are. They got a lot of good breaks." He paused again and added: "Some of them don't seem to know that. But it's true. Look at me. I hope I'm doing a good job, but I had a lot of luck."

Let us now return to the hypothesis of *Yesterday*: because of the intrinsic quality of their songs, Beatlemania was inevitable. If people now heard "I Saw Her Standing There," "Let It Be," or "Hey Jude" for the first time, they would immediately recognize that they were hearing something extraordinary. It would not matter whether people heard such songs in 1954, 1964, 1974, 1984, 1994, 2004, or 2044. It would not matter if people heard those songs alone and at home, and in a way that could not possibly be affected by social influences, or if they heard those songs in groups consisting largely of people predisposed, for one or another reason, to like those songs.

On an alternative account, *Yesterday*'s hypothesis is far too simple; social influences in general and cascade effects in particular were crucial to the rise of Beatlemania. By itself, this alternative claim is too vague to be a testable hypothesis; it could take various forms. On the weakest (and perhaps trivial) version, the Beatles' success was indeed inevitable in light of their genius, but it occurred in the precise way that it did, and with the speed it did, because they received the equivalent of a large number of early downloads.

On that view, there are plausible counterfactual worlds in which the Beatles ultimately succeeded, just as in our world, but in which that success unfolded at different speeds and in intriguingly different ways. This claim is indeed relatively trivial, and we should be immediately able to see why. Indeed, it is consistent with what I have called the hypothesis of *Yesterday*.

A stronger version is much bolder and not at all trivial. On that view, there is a counterfactual world in which the Beatles did not get the equivalent of a large number of initial downloads, and they ultimately gave up. In that counterfactual world, the Beatles might have been the equivalent of "Trapped in an Orange Peel," writ large. That world would be something like the world of *Yesterday*. Indeed, it might actually *be* the world of *Yesterday* (which never explains why, exactly, the Beatles never made it there). If so, the mystery of the movie would be simple to state if not to solve: Why would the Beatles' songs do spectacularly well now, when the group failed in the 1960s?

The plausibility of the bolder account is difficult to test, because (one last time) history is only run once. Before we investigate it, consider the remarkable words of one of Paul McCartney's best biographers: "The Beatles weren't only the greatest pop band in history; they were arguably also the luckiest."[1] On this account, the Beatles had at least two incredible strokes of good fortune, without which they would not have made it. The first was the acquisition of Brian Epstein as their manager; the second was Epstein's stumbling on George Martin, who became their producer. Those were indeed essential bits of good fortune, but they do not come close to exhausting the many happenstances, large and small, that turned the Beatles into the iconic Beatles.

With respect to the Beatles, we do not have anything like a randomized controlled trial, or a number of counterfactual worlds. The best and perhaps the only way to assess whether and in what sense the group's success was inevitable is through close investigation of the actual history—the only one we have—in search of clues. There are many such investigations. I shall pay attention to several of them and above all to the elaborate discussion by Mark Lewisohn, whose terrific book captures a series of serendipitous events that made the group's success possible, and which gestures toward counterfactual worlds in which Beatlemania would have never come into existence.[2] In a sense, we could read Lewisohn's account of the Beatles' rise as a temporally compressed cousin to Jackson's study of literary reputation.

As Lewisohn and others describe in detail (and intriguingly, the accounts are not precisely the same), the young group initially became quite popular in local clubs in Liverpool but struggled mightily to attract wider attention.[3] Social influences and other factors were not (sufficiently) in their favor. Lacking a manager, and with only modest prospects, they came pretty close to splitting up in 1961, fearing they were unlikely to succeed.[4] Eventually they asked two young secretaries, who were helping to run their Liverpool fan club, to manage the group. But the secretaries found it hard to get them bookings.

Young Beatles

Source: Bernard Gotfryd, *The Beatles, The Ed Sullivan Show [New York]*, 1964.

The group's initial break came when Brian Epstein, the twenty-seven-year-old manager of a Liverpool record store, happened to come hear them at a lunchtime session at a club. Epstein loved them and decided they would be "bigger than Elvis."[5] Improbably, he offered to manage them. He did so even though he lacked relevant experience and even though the Beatles had become unpopular with promoters and were, in Lewisohn's words, "damaged goods," known for "being unreliable, unpunctual, arrogant."[6]

At first Epstein's efforts proved futile. EMI, a prominent British recording company, refused to give the Beatles a contract. Epstein obtained an opportunity for them to test for Decca, EMI's rival. When they came to the studio, they did pretty well, but Decca's people thought that they lacked focus. It did not help that they came from Liverpool, which was far from London.⁷ "The boys won't go," the company's representatives informed Epstein.⁸

Instead of signing the Beatles, Decca chose to sign a butcher from London, Brian Poole, and his band, called the Tremeloes.⁹

The Beatles were stunned by Decca's rejection. John Lennon said they thought "that was the end."¹⁰ In Paul McCartney's words, "It was all a bit bloody hell, what are we gonna do?"¹¹ Epstein ended up seeing every potential record company, and *every one of them refused to sign the Beatles*. When Epstein kept saying that his group would be bigger than Elvis, studio executives thought he was daft. Pointing to his family's electrical stores, one of the executives said, "You've *got* a good business, Mr. Epstein. Why not stick to it?"¹²

In apparent desperation, Epstein went back to EMI, where he played a Beatles tape for producer George Martin, who was unimpressed. Martin saw "a rather raw group" with "a pretty lousy tape" and "not very good songs."¹³ That might have concluded matters except for the intervention of two people, Kim Bennett and Sid Colman, who worked for one of EMI's music publishing companies. Epstein had played some Beatles music for Bennett and Colman, who liked what they heard. In a highly unusual move, Colman offered to pay EMI for the cost of recording a Beatles record. But the resulting session, overseen by an unenthusiastic Martin, went poorly, and he decided not to issue any of the songs. He later confessed, "I didn't think the Beatles had any songs of any worth. They gave me no evidence whatsoever that they could write hit material."¹⁴

When the group came back into the studio, he did not like them much better, but he reluctantly concluded that "Love Me Do" could be released as a single. In doing so, Martin made a remarkable decision, one that perhaps would not have been made by any other

British producer: he chose to record Lennon-McCartney originals, rather than covers.[15] Still, he had little confidence in "Love Me Do," and when he mentioned the group's bizarre name to his EMI colleagues, they broke out in laughter.

EMI refused to support the song. Essentially all of the company's leaders found the song baffling.[16] They thought that it was a comedy record. In Martin's words, "Nobody believed in it at all."[17] When the song was released, it was hardly promoted. The disc jockeys who played it thought that it must have been a joke, thinking that a group named "the Beatles" could not be expected to be serious. Even in Liverpool, the group's fans were disappointed that the song did not seem to match their onstage personality.

"Love Me Do" might have dropped like a stone, along with the Beatles' prospects, except for Epstein's relentlessness. Epstein recruited a public relations team of his own, with the specific goal of promoting the song; he used his own money for that purpose.[18] A prominent part of the team was one Tony Calder, just nineteen years old, who liked the record and insisted on circulating free promotional copies to England's main ballroom chains, Top Rank and Mecca.[19] According to one report, Epstein himself purchased ten thousand copies of the record to ensure that it would enter the top twenty.[20]

Lennon himself always claimed that that never happened, and it might well be true that word of mouth turned the trick. The group's enthusiastic fan base in Liverpool ended up buying the record and started an informational cascade. Despite mixed reviews, Calder's strategy worked; early on, the song was not much on radio or television, but it made its way onto the dance floors. As time went on, Epstein's pushing helped make the song into an unexpected hit. It was seen as a pop song, not a comedy single, and it peaked at number seventeen on the charts.[21] The Beatles received new invitations. They were asked to perform on regional television programs and also on national BBC radio.[22]

At that point, Martin, the original skeptic, decided to make use of their modest fame. As a follow-up, he asked them to record a new single, "Please Please Me," and he sped up the original ballad, in the manner of Roy Orbison, into a genuine rock song ("Whoa yeah!"). After the first take, Martin told them they had their first number one record.[23] Was he right?

Epstein worked relentlessly to get his group before the public. As one of Lennon's biographers put it, "All that set the Beatles apart from a hundred other pop acts with half a hit," at that stage, "was the tireless dedication and sheer chutzpah of their manager."[24] Epstein was able to book them on a popular Saturday show called *Thank Your Lucky Stars* (a good name, yes?), where they played "Please Please Me." The showing happened to occur during the heaviest snowfalls in nearly a hundred years—which meant that a lot of teenagers were inside and watching.[25] Within two months, the song did indeed hit the number one spot.

Not long thereafter, Martin made an astounding decision. He decided to ask the Beatles to record a real album, consisting mostly of Lennon-McCartney songs. The name of the album, of course, was "Please Please Me." It included "I Saw Her Standing There," "P.S. I Love You," and "Do You Want to Know a Secret?" Still, Martin had a problem. EMI was hardly sold on the Beatles, and the company was unwilling to spend much money on the endeavor. But Martin turned out, of course, to be a brilliant producer, perfectly matched to the fledgling group. It was hardly smooth sailing from there, but the group was essentially launched.

There are many paths to success, and in a host of counterfactual worlds, the Beatles might have found one even without

Epstein, Bennett, Colman, and Martin. Lennon himself thought so, insisting that the Beatles were the best group in the world (using expletives before *best* and *world*). "Believing that is what made us what we were," he said. "It was just a matter of time before everybody caught on."[26] Perhaps so; evidently John accepted the hypothesis of *Yesterday*.

But in hindsight, it is really easy to do that. The best accounts of the crucial period, when the Beatles' fate seemed highly uncertain, reveal the possibility of radically different counterfactual worlds, suggesting that the group's success was anything but foreordained. And as we have seen, the word "foreordained" raises many puzzles. It is necessary to know what we are holding constant, and what we are changing, in those counterfactual worlds. For example: What if Paul had met John at some other time? What if John had been in an especially sour mood on the fateful day? What if John had decided that he had no interest in Paul's young friend George? What if Brian Epstein had not gone to see them when he did? What if George Martin had been unmovable during those early, skeptical days?

It is important to emphasize that some of the serendipitous factors had nothing to do with social influences. Epstein's involvement and enthusiasm might have been essential. In fact I think they were; it is hard to see how the group would have found a path without him. But it would be a stretch to see it as the functional equivalent of early downloads. Also crucial, it seems, was the involvement of Bennett and Colman. Even so, and notably, a failure to obtain (sufficient) early popularity in 1961 almost doomed the Beatles. How close did it come? We do not know. In addition, something very much like a large number of early downloads for "Love Me Do" in 1963 made all the difference. Was it essential to the Beatles' success? If "Love Me Do" had tanked, would they have failed? We do not know that either.

Would it be possible, in this light, to imagine a counterfactual world in which the Beatles did not make it? A counterfactual world without the Beatles, and instead with other bandmanias—say, Kinksmania or Holliesmania?

These questions might seem preposterous. The Beatles' enduring success—their rediscovery by successive generations, their spectacular success in various years long after they broke up—can be taken to support the idea that they were unique, and that their uniqueness made their success essentially inevitable. There is the question of sheer quality, which is surely relevant; recall H. J. Jackson's scorecard (see chapter 5). To be sure, Ray Davies of the Kinks is inventive and original (consider "Lola"), and Graham Nash, originally of the Hollies, is better than good (consider "Our House"), but neither of them could be put in the same category as Lennon or McCartney.

But it is important to be careful on this topic, and on several different counts. First, Lennon and McCartney were not, in 1961 or even 1963, the Lennon and McCartney we now know. Their early success was almost certainly a necessary condition for the flowering of what we rightly see as their genius. With a lot of money and time, and a tremendous boost to their confidence, Lennon and McCartney did not have to scramble. They could innovate. They could experiment. They could become something very different from what they were before. Second, we do not know what Davies, Nash, or many others might have done, or might have been, if they had had the extraordinary success of the Beatles in the early 1960s.

Return to Connie Converse: If she had not stopped making music in 1961, what kind of music would she have made in the next decades? Her extraordinary originality, in that short period in which she was playing almost entirely to friends and family, raises a set of intriguing questions about what she would have done if she had been at the forefront of the folk music revival in those immensely fertile years. Who and what might she have become?

EPILOGUE

"Placed in Favourable Situations"

R ecall Jane Franklin's heartbreaking words to her brother Benjamin, lamenting the "Thousands of Boyles Clarks and Newtons" who "have Probably been lost to the world, and lived and died in Ignorans and meanness, merely for want of being Placed in favourable situations, and Injoying Proper Advantages."[1] Who is placed in unfavorable situations? Who faces disadvantages?

We might speak of an absence of education; Franklin herself was not allowed proper schooling. We might speak of poverty or an absence of economic opportunity. We might speak of an absence of parental support. We might speak of discrimination. Or we might speak more specifically, and less systematically, about the absence of a mentor, a helping hand, a nod of appreciation, a glimpse of something amazing, an infusion of money, a year off, a friend or family member who refuses to give up.

Epilogue

In the domain of innovation in general, social scientists, sounding a lot like Jane Franklin, refer to "Lost Einsteins"—those "who would have had highly impactful inventions had they been exposed to innovation in childhood."[2] The emphasis here is on demographic characteristics, such as race, gender, and socioeconomic status, and on the contributions of role models and network effects to success. Countless potential innovators, in science, business, and elsewhere, were born in a family that did not or could not help, did not find the right role models, were subjugated in some way, or did not benefit from networks. As a result, they never innovated. They lost life's lottery, or a series of smaller lotteries.[3]

If young Cassius Clay had not had his bicycle stolen, would he have become the most famous person in the world? Might there have been other athletes, even greater than Muhammad Ali, who never made it onto the public stage? Ali is my personal favorite, and so it pains me to say so, but of course the answer is yes.

There are lost da Vincis, lost Shakespeares, lost Miltons, lost Austens, lost Blakes, lost Stan Lees, and lost Bob Dylans. There are lost Edisons and lost Teslas (Nikola, not the car). There are plenty of them. They have been lost for a thousand and one different reasons.

A central goal of liberalism, and of the liberal political tradition, is to undo damaging forms of subjugation, which is why John Stuart Mill's *The Subjection of Women* is a canonical liberal text (and essential reading, not least for anti-liberals). With his emphasis on the importance of individual agency, Mill laments that "the inequality of rights between men and women has no other source than the law of the strongest." In a key passage, Mill writes:

[W]hat is the peculiar character of the modern world—the difference which chiefly distinguishes modern institutions, modern social ideas, modern life itself, from those of times long past? It is that human beings are no longer born to their place in life, and chained down by an inexorable bond to the place they are born to, but are free to employ their faculties, and such favorable chances as offer, to achieve the lot which may appear to them most desirable.[4]

Mill's argument here is more subtle than the context might suggest. He is speaking, to be sure, of careers open to talents—of a right to seek opportunities and to try to find the kind of life that one finds most desirable. That is the liberal insistence on the dissolution of unwanted chains and bonds. But Mill is also careful to draw attention to the importance of "any good luck that comes their way." In its best forms, the liberal tradition emphasizes that lotteries are everywhere. It points to the place of "good luck" and the multiple forms it takes. John Rawls's *A Theory of Justice* is the most sustained development of that point.

One of my central themes here is that if innovators have been lost, it is not only because of demographic characteristics, but also because of a host of other factors that did not work in their favor. Perhaps the Zeitgeist was not on their side. There might have been no wave for them to catch. They might not have found the right enemies, inspirations, or champions. They might not have been able to benefit from a network. Someone might not have given them a path, a smile at the right time, a word of encouragement, an idea, an infusion of energy, or a contract. As Jackson puts it, we might want to give "the Hunts and the Southeys another chance, as it was also mainly because of adventitious circumstances that they fell by the wayside."[5] We might want to give a lot of people another chance, and for exactly the same reason.

Epilogue

These claims might seem to point to a tragedy, even to countless tragedies—not only for those who have been lost, but also for those of us who have lost them, perhaps because they were never given an opportunity, perhaps because they were never given attention. In many ways, that is indeed tragic.

But it also points to a possibility, or perhaps an inspiration. Lost Einsteins, or lost Shakespeares and Miltons, might be found again. In fact, they are being found every day. They are being found in the same way that the *Mona Lisa*, Jane Austen, William Blake, John Keats, Robert Johnson, and Connie Converse were found again. And if we can stay alert to the fact of their existence among us, right now, many fewer will get lost in the first place.

NOTES

Prologue

1. James Barron, "Historic Hysterics: Witnesses to a Really Big Show," *New York Times*, February 7, 2014, https://www.nytimes.com/2014/02/08/nyregion/the-beatles-debut-on-ed-sullivan.html.

2. Ed Sullivan Show, https://www.edsullivan.com/artists/the-beatles/.

3. Poor Richard (Benjamin Franklin), *An Almanack for the Year of Christ* (Philadelphia: B. Franklin, 1734).

4. Samuel Johnson, "No. 118," in *The Rambler*, vol. 4 (London: J. Payne and J. Bouquet, 1752).

5. Samuel Johnson, "No. 21," in *The Rambler*, vol. 1 (London: J. Payne and J. Bouquet, 1752).

6. Samuel Johnson, "No. 106," in *The Rambler*, vol. 4 (London: J. Payne and J. Bouquet, 1752).

7. Johnson, "No. 106."

8. Samuel Johnson, "Preface," in *The Plays of William Shakespeare* (London: J. and R. Tonson, C. Corbet, H. Woodfall, J. Rivington, R. Baldwin, L. Hawes, Clark and Collins, W. Johnston, T. Caslon, T. Lownds, and the Executors of B. Dodd, 1765).

9. Johnson, "Preface."

10. "The 14th Academy Awards," Academy of Motion Picture Arts and Sciences, https://www.oscars.org/oscars/ceremonies/1942.

11. "Biography," Robert Johnson Blues Foundation, https://robertjohnsonbluesfoundation.org/biography/.

12. "Biography."

13. "Biography."

14. See Reggie Ugwu, "Overlooked No More: Robert Johnson, Bluesman Whose Life Was a Riddle," *New York Times*, September 25, 2019, https://www.nytimes.com/2019/09/25/obituaries/robert-johnson-overlooked.html.

15. See Jon Wilde, "Robert Johnson Revelation Tells Us to Put the Brakes on the Blues," *Guardian*, May 27, 2010, https://www.theguardian.com/music/musicblog/2010/may/27/robert-johnson-blues.

16. Bob Dylan, *Chronicles*, vol. 1 (New York: Simon & Schuster, 2004), 284.

17. Dylan, 282.

18. Dylan, 287.

Notes

19. Bruce Conforth and Gayle Dean Wardlow, *Up Jumped the Devil: The Real Life of Robert Johnson* (Chicago: Chicago Review Press, 2019); Tom Graves, *Crossroads* (Memphis: Devault-Graves Agency, 2017); Matt Frederick, *A Meeting at the Crossroads: Robert Johnson and the Devil* (Chickenfeet Press, 2022).

20. "Testimonials," Robert Johnson Blues Foundation, https://robertjohnson bluesfoundation.org/testimonials/.

21. For very different answers, see Harold Bloom, *The Western Canon: The Books and Schools of the Ages* (New York: Houghton Mifflin Harcourt, 1994); Dean Keith Simonton, *Greatness: Who Makes History and Why* (New York: Guilford Press, 1994).

Chapter 1

1. Maureen Cleave, "How Does a Beatle Live? John Lennon Lives Like This," *London Evening Standard*, March 4, 1966.

2. There is a difference, of course, between fame and success, even spectacular success. Not long ago, I met a philanthropist who is spectacularly wealthy; he isn't famous (and he doesn't want to be), and I am not going to name him, but he has had phenomenal success in business. If we measure success by eminence and influence, Frank Michelman is one of the most successful law professors I know; Matthew Rabin is one of the most successful economists I know; Jon Elster is one of the most successful political scientists I know. None of them is a household name, or even widely known outside of their own academic field. Some people who are famous have not achieved much, or become eminent, in any field; consider the stars of reality television shows. My main focus here is on fame, but I am occasionally going to speak of spectacular success as well, whether or not it is accompanied by fame.

3. There are actually two fallacies here, not one. The first fallacy is selecting on the dependent variable. Some feature that is common to successes may also be common among failures, which means that finding that it is common to successes does not show that it helps produce success. The second, and the more subtle, is selecting on the *independent* variable. Consider the claim that "dyslexia causes people to be successful." That claim might focus exclusively on successful people, and so pick a particular attribute (in this case dyslexia), which is rare even among successful people. "Any person or company can be characterized by many features (independent variables), yet emotionally satisfying narrative explanations emphasize just one or a few of them. Given a small set of successes, one can often find a feature that is common to them; and given a feature, one can often find a small set of successes that display it. However, a particular feature being common to a small, selected set of successes does not necessarily imply that it is common *even among successes*." George Lifchits et al., "Success Stories Cause False Beliefs about Success," *Judgment and Decision Making* 16, no. 6 (November 2021): 1439–1440.

4. Jim Collins, *Good to Great: Why Some Companies Make the Leap . . . and Others Don't* (New York: HarperBusiness, 2001).

5. Thomas J. Peters and Robert H. Waterman Jr., *In Search of Excellence* (New York: Collins Business Essentials, 2012).

6. See Dean Keith Simonton, *Greatness: Who Makes History and Why* (New York: Guilford Press, 1994).

7. See Lifchits, "Success Stories."

8. Donald Sassoon, *Mona Lisa: The History of the World's Most Famous Painting* (London: HarperCollins Publishers, 2001).

9. See "The Theft That Made the 'Mona Lisa' a Masterpiece," *All Things Considered*, NPR, July 30, 2011, https://www.npr.org/2011/07/30/138800110/the -theft-that-made-the-mona-lisa-a-masterpiece.

10. Duncan Watts, *Everything Is Obvious* (New York: Crown Business, 2011), 60. I have been greatly influenced by Watts's brilliant book, and I draw on his account here.

11. H. J. Jackson, *Those Who Write for Immortality* (New Haven: Yale University Press, 2015), xii–xiii.

12. See, e.g., Simonton, *Greatness*; Dean Keith Simonton, *Creativity in Science: Change, Logic, Genius, and Zeitgeist* (Cambridge: Cambridge University Press, 2004).

13. For its website, see *Journal of Genius and Eminence*, ICSC Press, https:// icscpress.com/journals/jge/.

14. See Simonton, *Greatness*, 227.

15. Dean Keith Simonton, "Philosophical Eminence, Beliefs, and Zeitgeist: An Individual-Generational Analysis," *Journal of Personality and Social Psychology* 34, no. 4 (1976): 630–640.

16. See Dean Keith Simonton, "Cinematic Success Criteria and Their Predictors," *Psychology and Marketing* 26, no. 5 (May 2009): 400–420.

17. See Dean Keith Simonton, "Popularity, Content, and Context in 37 Shakespeare Plays," *Poetics* 15, no. 4 (1986): 493–510.

18. Simonton, *Greatness*, 138.

19. For an engaging discussion of one-hit wonders, and the role of chance in their single hits, see Aaron Kozbelt, "One Hit Wonders in Classical Music: Evidence and (Partial) Explanations for an Early Career Peak," *Creativity Research Journal* 20, no. 2 (2008): 179–195.

20. Robert Shelton, "Bob Dylan: A Distinctive Folk-Song Stylist," *New York Times*, September 29, 1961.

21. John Maynard Keynes, *The General Theory of Employment, Interest and Money* (London: Macmillan, 1936), 113–114.

22. John Maynard Keynes, "The General Theory of Employment," *Quarterly Journal of Economics* 51, no. 2 (February 1937): 212, 213.

23. Keynes, 212, 213.

24. Keynes, 212, 213.

Notes

25. Matthew J. Salganik et al., "Measuring the Predictability of Life Outcomes with a Scientific Mass Collaboration," *Proceedings of the National Academy of Sciences (PNAS)* 117, no. 15 (April 2020): 8398–8403.

26. Salganik, "Predictability of Life Outcomes."

27. Salganik, "Predictability of Life Outcomes."

28. Salganik, "Predictability of Life Outcomes."

Chapter 2

1. See Howard Fishman, *To Anyone Who Ever Asks: The Life, Music, and Mystery of Connie Converse* (New York: Dutton, 2023).

2. Fishman, 329.

3. Fishman, 329.

4. Fishman, 328.

5. Fishman, 26.

6. Fishman, 485.

7. Fishman, 445.

8. Matthew J. Salganik, Peter Sheridan Dodds, and Duncan J. Watts, "Experimental Study of Inequality and Unpredictability in an Artificial Cultural Market," *Science* 311, no. 5762 (February 2006): 854–856.

9. The Music Lab experiment has inspired a large literature. For a finding that early success produces large initial improvements that dwindle over time, see Arnout van de Rijt et al., "Field Experiments of Success-Breeds-Success Dynamics," *Proceedings of the National Academy of Sciences (PNAS)* 111, no. 19 (April 2014): 6934–6939. For an instructive reanalysis of the Music Lab experiment, finding that superior alternatives gained in popularity, alongside self-correcting dynamics in a new experiment, see Arnout van de Rijt, "Self-Correcting Dynamics in Social Influence Processes," *American Journal of Sociology* 124, no. 5 (March 2019): 1468–1495. For a valuable effort to separate various effects, including effects of social signals, see Tad Hogg and Kristina Lerman, "Disentangling the Effects of Social Signals," *Human Computation* 2, no. 2 (2015): 189–208. For an important and intriguing finding that predictive models do well if they "peek" into "early adopters and properties of their social networks spanning music, books, photos, and URLs," see Benjamin Shulman, Amit Sharma, and Dan Cosley, "Predictions of Popularity: Gaps between Prediction and Understanding," *Proceedings of the International AAAI Conference on Web and Social Media* 10, no. 1 (2016): 348–357. Rijt's findings in particular offer some cautionary notes about the broadest readings of the Music Lab experiment, but I do not believe that they are inconsistent with the use I make of that experiment here. (For the defense, I call Herman Melville, Vincent Van Gogh, Jane Austen, William Blake, John Keats, and Robert Johnson as my first witnesses.)

10. Michael Macy, Sebastian Deri, Alexander Ruch, and Natalie Tong, "Opinion Cascades and the Unpredictability of Partisan Polarization," *Science Advances* 5, no. 8 (August 2019): 1–7.

11. Ziv Epstein et al., "Social Influence Leads to the Formation of Diverse Local Trends," *Proceedings of the ACM on Human-Computer Interaction* 5, no. CSCW2 (October 2021): 1–18.

12. See Jason Cohen, "iOS More Popular in Japan and US, Android Dominates in China and India," *PC Mag*, September 4, 2020, https://www.pcmag.com/news/ios-more-popular-in-japan-and-us-android-dominates-in-china-and-india.

13. See Katie McLaughlin, "Fleetwood Mac's 'Rumours' at 35: Still the 'Perfect Album,'" CNN, June 27, 2012, http://edition.cnn.com/2012/06/26/showbiz/fleetwood-mac-rumours/index.html.

14. See Lindsey Buckingham, Stevie Nicks, and Christine McVie, interview, 1977, https://www.youtube.com/watch?v=lLaWDjNLC_4.

15. Buckingham, Nicks, and McVie, interview.

16. Buckingham, Nicks, and McVie, interview.

17. Buckingham, Nicks, and McVie, interview.

18. Mark Olsen, "Oscars 2013: 'Searching for Sugar Man' Wins Best Documentary," *Los Angeles Times*, February 24, 2013, https://www.latimes.com/entertainment/envelope/la-xpm-2013-feb-24-la-et-mn-oscars-2013-best-documentary-20130220-story.html.

19. "JK Rowling's Crime Novel Becomes Bestseller," *Guardian*, July 15, 2013, https://www.theguardian.com/books/2013/jul/15/jk-rowling-cuckoos-calling-bestseller.

Chapter 3

1. See Colin Martindale, "Fame More Fickle Than Fortune: On the Distribution of Literary Eminence," *Poetics* 23, no. 3 (1995): 219–234.

2. Martindale, "Fame More Fickle."

3. Martindale, "Fame More Fickle."

4. Martindale, "Fame More Fickle."

5. Robert K. Merton, "The Matthew Effect in Science," *Science* 159, no. 3810 (January 1968): 56–63.

6. David Easley and Jon Kleinberg, *Networks, Crowds, and Markets: Reasoning about a Highly Connected World* (New York: Cambridge University Press, 2010), 483.

7. Merton, "The Matthew Effect in Science."

8. Merton, 58.

9. Merton, 59.

10. Merton, 62.

11. Easley and Kleinberg, *Networks, Crowds, and Markets*, 549–550.

12. See Anna Collar, *Religious Networks in the Roman Empire: The Spread of New Ideas* (Cambridge: Cambridge University Press, 2014).

13. Easley and Kleinberg, *Networks, Crowds, and Markets*, 426.

Notes

14. Matthew J. Salganik and Duncan J. Watts, "Leading the Herd Astray: An Experimental Study of Self-Fulfilling Prophecies in an Artificial Cultural Market," *Social Psychology Quarterly* 71, no. 4 (2008): 338–355.

15. See Salganik and Watts, "Leading the Herd Astray."

16. See Hans Luijten, *Jo van Gogh-Bonger: The Woman Who Made Vincent Famous* (London: Bloomsbury, 2022).

17. Cass R. Sunstein, Reid Hastie, and David Schkade, "What Happened on Deliberation Day," *California Law Review* 95, no. 3 (June 2007): 915–940.

18. Sunstein, Hastie, and Schkade, 930.

19. See Roger Brown, *Social Psychology*, 2d ed. (New York: Free Press, 1986), 224.

20. David G. Myers, "Discussion-Induced Attitude Polarization," *Human Relations* 28, no. 8 (1975): 699–714.

21. David G. Myers and George D. Bishop, "Discussion Effects on Racial Attitudes," *Science* 169, no. 3947 (1970): 779.

22. Myers and Bishop, 779.

23. Richard J. Butler, Benjamin W. Cowan, and Sebastian Nilsson, "From Obscurity to Bestseller: Examining the Impact of Oprah's Book Club Selections," *Publishing Research Quarterly* 20, no. 4 (Winter 2005): 23–34.

24. See Howard Markel, "Truman Capote's Unhappy Ending," *NewsHour*, PBS, October 1, 2022, https://www.pbs.org/newshour/health/truman-capotes -unhappy-ending.

25. Michela Ponzo and Vincenzo Scoppa, "Famous after Death: The Effect of a Writer's Death on Book Sales," *Journal of Economic Behavior and Organization* 210 (June 2023): 210–225.

26. See David Maddison and Anders Jul Pedersen, "The Death Effect in Art Prices: Evidence from Denmark," *Applied Economics* 40, no. 14 (2008): 1789–1793; see also R. B. Ekelund Jr. et al., "The 'Death-Effect' in Art Prices: A Demand-Side Exploration," *Journal of Cultural Economics* 24, no. 4 (2000): 283–300.

27. Dean Talbot, "Number of Books Published Per Year," WordsRated, February 2, 2022, https://wordsrated.com/number-of-books-published-per-year -2021/. This might be an overestimate, for reasons that are too boring to discuss here.

28. See "Death Rate, Crude (per 1,000 People)," The World Bank, https://data .worldbank.org/indicator/SP.DYN.CDRT.IN.

Chapter 4

1. See Jill Lepore, *Book of Ages: The Life and Opinions of Jane Franklin* (New York: Vintage Books, 2014), 218.

2. Lepore, 218.

3. See Lepore, xi.

4. Virginia Woolf, *A Room of One's Own* (London: Hogarth Press, 1929), 46–47.

5. Jeanne Peijnenburg and Sander Verhaegh, "Analytic Women," *Aeon*, August 1, 2023, https://aeon.co/essays/the-lost-women-of-early-analytic-philosophy.

6. See Jeanne Peijnenburg and Sander Verhaegh, *Women in the History of Analytic Philosophy* (Cham: Springer, 2022).

7. George Orwell, *1984* (New York: Harcourt, Brace, 1949), 195.

8. See Maurice Halbwachs, *On Collective Memory*, trans. and ed. Lewis A. Coser (Chicago: University of Chicago Press, 1992).

9. Halbwachs, 21–22.

10. Orwell, *1984*, 195.

11. A brilliant discussion is Géraldine Schwarz, *Those Who Forget*, trans. Laura Marris (New York: Scribner, 2020). Don't not read it.

12. Halbwachs, *On Collective Memory*, 234.

13. Halbwachs, 234.

14. Halbwachs, 92.

15. Halbwachs, 94.

16. Halbwachs, 94.

17. Halbwachs, 95.

18. Halbwachs, 101.

19. Halbwachs, 102.

20. Aleida Assmann, "Canon and Archive," in *Cultural Memory Studies*, ed. Astrid Erll and Ansgar Nünning (Berlin: Walter de Gruyter, 2008), 97.

21. Halbwachs, *On Collective Memory*, 107.

22. Halbwachs, 115.

23. See Elaine Pagels, *The Gnostic Gospels* (New York: Vintage Books, 1989).

24. Halbwachs, *On Collective Memory*, 203. For a valuable collection, see Astrid Erll and Ansgar Nünning, eds., *Cultural Memory Studies* (Berlin: Walter de Gruyter, 2008).

25. For one of my favorites, see Robert Charles Wilson, *Mysterium* (New York: Orb, 2010).

26. See John K. Papadopoulos, "Canon Creation/Destruction and Cultural Formation: Authority, Reception, Canonicity, Marginality," in *Canonisation as Innovation*, eds. Damien Agut-Labordère and Miguel John Versluys (Leiden: Brill, 2022), 3. A valuable overview is Lee Martin McDonald, *The Formation of the Biblical Canon*, vol. 2, *The New Testament: Its Authority and Canonicity* (London: Bloomsbury T&T Clark, 2021).

27. McDonald, 350.

28. McDonald, 7.

29. McDonald, 351.

30. McDonald, 4.

31. Pagels, *The Gnostic Gospels*, 142.

Notes

32. McDonald, *The Formation of the Biblical Canon,* vol. 2, 219.

33. See Herbert Grabes, "Cultural Memory and the Literary Canon," in *Cultural Memory Studies,* eds. Astrid Erll and Ansgar Nünning (Berlin: Walter de Gruyter, 2008), 311; Robert von Hallberg, ed., *Canons* (Chicago: University of Chicago Press, 1984).

34. See Sandra Lapoint and Erich Reck, eds., *Historiography and the Formation of Philosophical Canons* (New York: Routledge, 2023).

35. For discussion, see Ralf von Appen and Andre Doehring, "Nevermind the Beatles, Here's Exile 61 and Nico: 'The Top 100 Records of All Time'—A Canon of Pop and Rock Albums from a Sociological and an Aesthetic Perspective," *Popular Music* 25, no. 1 (January 2006): 21–39. This essay finds a great deal of stability, which can be taken to be a tribute to the persistence of cascade effects, a tribute to the power of sheer quality, or a tribute to the Beatles.

36. Harold Bloom, *The Western Canon: The Books and Schools of the Ages* (New York: Houghton Mifflin Harcourt, 1994), 27.

37. Bloom, 27.

38. See Hugh Kenner, "The Making of the Modernist Canon," in *Canons,* ed. Robert von Hallberg (Chicago: University of Chicago Press, 1984), 363.

39. Preface to the First Folio, http://www.shakespeare-online.com/biography /firstfolio.html.

40. Gerard Manley Hopkins, "Spring and Fall." *Gerard Manley Hopkins: Poems and Prose* (Penguin Classics, 1985).

41. Bloom, *The Western Canon,* 27–28.

42. For relevant discussion, see Gillian Gualtiari, "Canonized Women and Women Canonizers: Gender Dynamics in *The Norton Anthology of English Literature*'s Eight Editions," *Gender Issues* 28 (2011): 94–109; Sean Shesgreen, "Canonizing the Canonizer: A Short History of The Norton Anthology of English Literature," *Critical Inquiry* 35, no. 2 (Winter 2009): 293–318. On the general issue, see John Guillary, *Cultural Capital: The Problem of Literary Canon Formation* (Chicago: University of Chicago Press, 1993); Bloom, *The Western Canon.*

43. Michelle Levy and Mark Perry, "Distantly Reading the Romantic Canon: Quantifying Gender in Current Anthologies," *Women's Writing* 22, no. 2 (2015): 136.

44. Gualtiari, "Canonized Women and Women Canonizers," 95.

45. Shesgreen, "Canonizing the Canonizer," 315–316.

46. Ken Gewertz, "Greenblatt Edits 'Norton Anthology,'" *Harvard Gazette,* February 2, 2006, https://news.harvard.edu/gazette/story/2006/02/greenblatt -edits-norton-anthology/.

47. I am exaggerating. I hope. See Bloom, *The Western Canon.*

48. See Bloom, 3.

Chapter 5

1. Leigh Hunt, "Jenny Kiss'd Me." *Poetry Foundation,* November 1938, https://www.poetryfoundation.org/poems/50495/jenny-kissd-me. Accessed November 2023.

2. Leigh Hunt, "Jenny Kiss'd Me."

3. See H. J. Jackson, *Those Who Write for Immortality* (New Haven: Yale University Press, 2015).

4. Jackson, 114.

5. Jackson, 115.

6. Jackson, 161.

7. Jackson, 117.

8. Jackson, 116.

9. Jackson, 115.

10. Jackson, 117.

11. Jackson, 118.

12. Jackson, 120.

13. Jackson, 122.

14. Jackson, 125.

15. Jackson, 125.

16. Jackson, 127.

17. Jackson, 156.

18. Jackson, 155.

19. Jackson, 161.

20. Jackson, 163.

21. Jackson, 163.

22. Jackson, 163.

23. Jackson, 40–41.

24. Jackson, 112.

25. Steve Jones and Joli Jensen, eds., *Afterlife as Afterimage: Understanding Posthumous Fame* (New York: P. Lang, 2005), xix.

26. Jackson, *Those Who Write for Immortality*, 113.

27. Jackson, 113.

28. Jackson, 113.

29. Jackson, 114.

30. Jackson, 131.

31. Jackson, 85.

32. Jackson, 85.

33. Quoted in Jackson, 86.

34. Jackson, 87.

35. Jackson, 88.

36. Jackson, 88.

37. Jackson, 91–92.

38. Jackson, 95.

39. Jackson, 95.

40. See Devoney Looser, *The Making of Jane Austen* (Baltimore: Johns Hopkins University Press, 2017), 2.

41. Looser, 4.

42. Looser, 6.
43. Looser, 4.
44. Jackson, *Those Who Write for Immortality*, 96.
45. Jackson, 98.
46. Looser, *The Making of Jane Austen*, 19.
47. Looser, 20.
48. Jackson, *Those Who Write for Immortality*, 101.
49. See Looser, *The Making of Jane Austen*, 75.
50. Jackson, *Those Who Write for Immortality*, 104.
51. Jackson, 104.
52. Jackson, 105.
53. William Blake, "Jerusalem," *Preface to Milton: A Poem in Two Books* (1810).
54. William Blake, "Jerusalem."
55. Jackson, *Those Who Write for Immortality*, 168.
56. Jackson, 168.
57. Jackson, 172.
58. Jackson, 168.
59. Jackson, 177.
60. Jackson, 183.
61. Jackson, 183.
62. Jackson, 162.
63. Jackson, 218.
64. Jackson, 166.
65. Gladys Engel Lang and Kurt Lang have studied the posthumous durability of art, with particular reference to etching. See Gladys Engel Lang and Kurt Lang, "Recognition and Renown: The Survival of Artistic Reputation," *American Journal of Sociology* 94, no. 1 (July 1988): 79–109. Their starting point is the idea of "collective memory," studied in sociology. They ask: "Why is it that the names of some persons, and the accomplishments on which their reputations rest, are more widely remembered than those of others once similarly acclaimed?" The link with Jackson's work could not be clearer.

Lang and Lang "do not dispute the influence of the deed on what people will remember about the doer." But in their view, the differences among the top performers are small, and yet we observe large differences in levels of acclaim. This is, of course, the Matthew Effect. Lang and Lang draw attention to the role of sociological factors, including "supposedly extraneous influences," in producing disparities in survival in collective memory. Studying a large data set, they find that it is important for artists to have "survivors with an emotional or financial stake in the perpetuation of their reputations." Close family greatly matters, and when artists do not have one, friends and admirers can make all the difference. Lang and Lang also emphasize the importance of "networks and circles."

66. Leigh Hunt, "Song of Fairies Robbing an Orchard." *Poetry Foundation*, 1938, https://www.poetryfoundation.org/poems/44436/song-of-fairies-robbing -an-orchard. Accessed November 2023.

Chapter 6

1. J. W. Rinzler, *The Making of Star Wars* (New York: Ballantine Books, 2007), 294.

2. Rinzler, 295.

3. Chris Taylor, *How Star Wars Conquered the Universe* (New York: Basic Books, 2014), 182; Rinzler, 294.

4. See Michael Coate, "The Original First-Week Engagements of 'Star Wars,'" *in70mm*, May 25, 2003, https://www.in70mm.com/presents/1963_blow _up/titel/s/star_wars/index.htm.

5. Taylor, *How Star Wars Conquered the Universe*, 187.

6. Rinzler, *The Making of Star Wars*, 304.

7. Michael Zoldessy, "Celebrating the Original Star Wars on Its 35th Anniversary," *Cinema Treasures*, May 25, 2012, http://cinematreasures.org/blog /2012/5/25/celebrating-the-original-star-wars-on-its-35th-anniversary.

8. Zoldessy, "Celebrating the Original Star Wars."

9. Rinzler, *The Making of Star Wars*, 304.

10. Rinzler, 304.

11. Rinzler, 302.

12. Rinzler, 300.

13. See "Star Wars: Episode IV—A New Hope," Box Office Mojo, https://www .boxofficemojo.com/title/tt0076759/?ref_=bo_se_r_1.

14. See "Feature Film, Released between 1977-01-01 and 1977-12-31 (Sorted by US Box Office Descending)," IMDb, https://www.imdb.com/search/title /?title_type=feature&year=1977-01-01,1977-12-31&sort=boxoffice_gross_us,desc.

15. See "Feature Film, Released between 1977-01-01 and 1977-12-31."

16. "Top Lifetime Adjusted Grosses," Box Office Mojo, https://www .boxofficemojo.com/chart/top_lifetime_gross_adjusted/?adjust_gross_to=2019.

17. See "Top Lifetime Adjusted Grosses."

18. See "GDP (current US$)—Samoa," World Bank, https://data.worldbank .org/indicator/NY.GDP.MKTP.CD?locations=WS.

19. See "Franchise: Star Wars," Box Office Mojo, https://www.boxofficemojo .com/franchise/fr3125251845/.

20. See "Top Lifetime Adjusted Grosses."

21. Paul Scanlon, "George Lucas: The Wizard of 'Star Wars,'" *Rolling Stone*, August 25, 1977, https://www.rollingstone.com/feature/george-lucas-the-wizard -of-star-wars-2-232011/.

22. Rinzler, *The Making of Star Wars*, 36.

23. Rinzler, 36.

24. Scanlon, "George Lucas: The Wizard of 'Star Wars.'"

25. Taylor, *How Star Wars Conquered the Universe*, 156.

26. Kirsten Acuna, "George Lucas Was Convinced 'Star Wars' Would Be a Disaster until This Phone Call in 1977," *Business Insider*, April 18, 2015,

https://www.yahoo.com/entertainment/news/first-time-george-lucas-understood
-140554197.html.

27. Acuna.

28. Taylor, *How Star Wars Conquered the Universe*, 184.

29. Taylor, 156–157.

30. Sally Kline, ed., *George Lucas: Interviews* (Jackson, MS: University Press of Mississippi, 1999), 81.

31. Scanlon, "George Lucas: The Wizard of 'Star Wars.'"

32. Taylor, *How Star Wars Conquered the Universe*, 157. I draw at various points here on Taylor's superb treatment.

33. Mike Musgrove, "Review: 'How Star Wars Conquered the Universe,' by Chris Taylor," *Washington Post*, October 10, 2014, https://www.washingtonpost
.com/entertainment/books/review-how-star-wars-conquered-the-universe-by
-chris-taylor/2014/10/09/6cd5afa2-32bc-11e4-8f02-03c644b2d7d0_story.html.

34. Taylor, *How Star Wars Conquered the Universe*, 187.

35. Susana Polo, "Stephen Colbert and George Lucas Talk Star Wars, Wooden Dialogue and Howard the Duck," *Polygon*, April 18, 2015, https://www.polygon
.com/2015/4/18/8448685/stephen-colbert-george-lucas-tribeca-talk.

36. *When Star Wars Ruled the World*, aired September 18, 2004, on VH1.

37. *When Star Wars Ruled the World*.

38. Gavin Edwards, "The Many Faces of Vader," *Rolling Stone*, June 2, 2005, https://www.rollingstone.com/tv-movies/tv-movie-news/the-many-faces-of
-vader-67888/.

39. *When Star Wars Ruled the World*.

40. Carrie Fisher, "The Arrival of the Jedi," *Time*, March 31, 2003, https://
content.time.com/time/specials/packages/article/0,28804,1977881_1977891
_1978545,00.html.

41. Taylor, *How Star Wars Conquered the Universe*, 145.

42. Polo, "Stephen Colbert and George Lucas Talk Star Wars."

43. Paul Young, "Star Wars (1977)," in *Fifty Key American Films*, eds. John White and Sabine Haenni (New York: Routledge, 2009), 180.

44. Rinzler, *The Making of Star Wars*, 247.

45. Rinzler, 256.

46. Rinzler, 288.

47. Taylor, *How Star Wars Conquered the Universe*, 184.

48. Rinzler, *The Making of Star Wars*, 297.

49. Vincent Canby, "'Star Wars'—A Trip to a Far Galaxy That's Fun and Funny," *New York Times*, May 26, 1977, https://www.nytimes.com/1977/05/26
/archives/star-wars-a-trip-to-a-far-galaxy-thats-fun-and-funny.html.

50. See Taylor, *How Star Wars Conquered the Universe*, 164.

51. Joseph Gelmis, "Superb Sci-Fi," *Newsday*, May 27, 1977, https://www
.newsday.com/entertainment/movies/star-wars-newsday-s-original-1977-movie
-review-f53771.

52. Taylor, *How Star Wars Conquered the Universe*, 187.

53. "The 50th Academy Awards," Academy of Motion Picture Arts and Sciences, https://www.oscars.org/oscars/ceremonies/1978/S?qt-honorees=1#block -quicktabs-honorees.

54. "'Star Wars': Their First Time," *New York Times*, October 28, 2015, https:// www.nytimes.com/interactive/2015/10/28/movies/star-wars-memories.html.

55. Rinzler, *The Making of Star Wars*, 298.

56. Rinzler, 298.

57. Jonathan Lethem, "13, 1977, 21," in *A Galaxy Not So Far Away*, ed. Glenn Kenny (New York: Holt, 2015), 1.

58. Todd Hansen, "A Big Dumb Movie about Space Wizards: Struggling to Cope with *The Phantom Menace*," in *A Galaxy Not So Far Away*, ed. Glenn Kenny (New York: Holt, 2015), 181.

59. Gary Arnold, "'Star Wars': A Spectacular Intergalactic Joyride," *Washington Post*, May 25, 1977, https://www.washingtonpost.com/news/arts-and -entertainment/wp/2015/12/20/how-does-the-original-1977-star-wars-review -from-the-washington-post-hold-up/.

60. See *Time*, May 30, 1977, https://content.time.com/time/magazine /0,9263,7601770530,00.html.

61. Rinzler, *The Making of Star Wars*, 195–196.

62. Rinzler, 297.

63. Rinzler, 297.

64. Arion Berger, "A Night Out at the Memeplex," in *A Galaxy Not So Far Away*, ed. Glenn Kenny (New York: Holt, 2015), 64.

65. Ann Friedman, "You Can't Miss a Universal Event," *Akron Beacon Journal*, December 29, 2015, https://www.beaconjournal.com/story/opinion /columns/2015/12/29/ann-friedman-you-can-t/10718665007/.

66. Berger, "A Night Out at the Memeplex," 66.

67. Taylor, *How Star Wars Conquered the Universe*, 187 n.4.

68. Rinzler, *The Making of Star Wars*, 297.

69. Taylor, *How Star Wars Conquered the Universe*, 189.

70. Taylor, 189.

71. Taylor, 189.

72. *Star Wars: The Legacy Revealed*, aired May 28, 2007, on History Channel.

73. Friedman, "You Can't Miss a Universal Event."

74. A. O. Scott, "How 'Star Wars' Defined My Generation," *New York Times*, October 28, 2015, https://www.nytimes.com/2015/11/01/movies/star-wars-elvis -and-me.html.

75. Taylor, *How Star Wars Conquered the Universe*, 163.

76. David Wilkinson, *The Power of the Force* (Oxford: Lion, 2000), 67–69.

77. *Star Wars: The Legacy Revealed*.

78. *Star Wars: The Legacy Revealed*.

Notes

79. President Jimmy Carter, Report to the American People on Energy (February 2, 1977), https://www.nytimes.com/1977/02/03/archives/the-text-of -jimmy-carters-first-presidential-report-to-the-american.html.

Chapter 7

1. See "Brand: Marvel Comics," Box Office Mojo, https://www.boxofficemojo .com/brand/bn3732077058/.

2. "Brand: Marvel Comics."

3. "Brand: Marvel Comics."

4. See "Stan Lee," Encyclopedia Britannica, https://www.britannica.com /biography/Stan-Lee.

5. Megan McCluskey, "These Are Some of the Most Beloved Heroes and Villains You'd Never Know without Stan Lee," *Time*, November 12, 2018, https:// time.com/5452364/stan-lee-marvel-characters/.

6. Bryce Morris, "Stan Lee's First Marvel Fan Club Paved the Way for Modern Fandom," *Screen Rant*, August 28, 2021, https://screenrant.com/stan -lee-merry-marvel-marching-society-fan-club/.

7. Michael Cavna, "'The Avengers' to 'Spider-Man': Nearing 90, Marvel Mastermind Stan Lee Shoots from the Still-Hip (About Whedon, Kirby, and RDJ)," *Washington Post*, May 3, 2012, https://www.washingtonpost.com/blogs /comic-riffs/post/the-avengers-to-spider-man-nearing-90-marvelmastermind-stan -lee-shoots-from-the-still-hip-about-whedon-kirbyand-rdj/2018/11/12/9011abfe -94d2-11e1-ac40-12b3c15489c0_blog.html.

8. Cavna.

9. Percy Bysshe Shelley, "A Defence of Poetry," in *Essays, Letters from Abroad, Translations and Fragments, by Percy Bysshe Shelley*, ed. Mary Wollstonecraft Shelley (London: Edward Moxon, 1840), 86.

10. The tale I tell here has been told by many people, including Lee himself, and in many places. It is sometimes told somewhat differently; I offer what seems to me to be the most plausible account, or at least not less plausible than the alternatives. Two excellent discussions, from which I have learned a great deal, are Liel Leibovitz, *Stan Lee: A Life in Comics* (New Haven: Yale University Press, 2020); and Reed Tucker, *Slugfest: Inside the Epic, 50-Year Battle between Marvel and DC* (New York: Da Capo Press, 2017). For some of the events and quotations in this chapter, I have drawn on Leibovitz's superb book; I economize on footnotes and offer this note as a general acknowledgment.

11. Tucker, *Slugfest*, xii.

12. Tucker, 16.

13. Leibovitz, *Stan Lee*, 1–2.

14. Tucker, *Slugfest*, 17.

15. Leibovitz, *Stan Lee*, 3.

16. Leibovitz, 34.

17. Richard Lea and Sian Cain, "Stan Lee: Spider-Man, X-Men and Avengers Creator Dies Aged 95," *Guardian*, November 12, 2018, https://www.theguardian .com/books/2018/nov/12/stan-lee-spider-man-x-men-avengers-marvel-universe -dies.

18. Lea and Cain.

19. Bruce Munro, "A True Marvel: How Stan Lee Led the 1960s Superhero Revolution," *BBC*, November 12, 2018, https://www.bbc.co.uk/programmes /articles/YdCRCCdSc6ZdBfoHl6mS5G/a-true-marvel-how-stan-lee-led-the-1960s -superhero-revolution.

20. Tucker, *Slugfest*, 19.

21. Leibovitz, *Stan Lee*, 93.

22. Leibovitz, 102.

23. See Matt Miller, "Stan Lee's Powerful 1968 Essay about the Evils of Racism Is Still Necessary Today," *Esquire*, November 12, 2018, https://www .esquire.com/entertainment/movies/a25022397/stan-lee-marvel-racism-1968 -essay/.

24. See Jef Rouner, "Stan Lee's Immortal Message about Politics in Pop Art," *Houston Press*, November 13, 2018, https://www.houstonpress.com/houston /Print?oid=11035025.

25. Tucker, *Slugfest*, 21.

26. Leibovitz, *Stan Lee*, 12.

27. See Joseph Campbell, *The Hero with a Thousand Faces* (New York: Meridian Books, 1949).

28. Campbell, 30.

29. Stan Lee (@TheRealStanLee), Twitter, November 9, 2010, 5:54 PM, https://twitter.com/TheRealStanLee/status/2131837090529280?lang=en.

30. Jim Beard, "Stan's Soapbox: Elevating Excelsior," *Marvel*, August 29, 2019, https://www.marvel.com/articles/culture-lifestyle/stan-s-soapbox -elevating-excelsior.

31. Tucker, *Slugfest*, 41.

32. Tucker, 23.

Chapter 8

1. A detailed discussion can be found in Tali Sharot and Cass R. Sunstein, *Look Again* (New York: Atria/One Signal Publishers, forthcoming).

2. See Daniel Simons et al., "Induced Visual Fading of Complex Images," *Journal of Vision* 6, no. 10 (2006): 1093–1101.

3. See, e.g., Paul Dolan, *Happiness by Design* (New York: Hudson Street Press, 2014).

4. Shigehiro Oishi and Erin C. Westgate, "A Psychologically Rich Life: Beyond Happiness and Meaning," *Psychological Review* 129, no. 4 (2022): 790–811.

Notes

5. See Oishi and Westgate, "A Psychologically Rich Life."

6. Jack Kerouac, *On the Road* (New York: Viking Press, 1957), 5.

7. See *No Direction Home*, directed by Martin Scorsese, aired September 27, 2005, on PBS.

8. See generally Bob Dylan, *The Philosophy of Modern Song* (New York: Simon & Schuster, 2022).

9. Jonathan Cott, ed., *Bob Dylan: The Essential Interviews* (New York: Wenner Books, 2006), 104.

10. Cott, 104.

11. See Joe Garza, "Bob Dylan's High School Yearbook Showed His Dreams of Musical Stardom Started Early," MSN, November 4, 2022, https://www.msn .com/en-us/music/news/bob-dylan-s-high-school-yearbook-showed-his-dreams -of-musical-stardom-started-early/ar-AA13KaBk?ocid=a2hs.

12. Curt Eriksmoen, "After a Summer in Fargo, Bob Dylan Went from Rock 'n' Roll Aspirant to Folk Music Legend," *Inforum*, March 20, 2021, https://www .inforum.com/lifestyle/arts-and-entertainment/after-a-summer-in-fargo-bob -dylan-went-from-rock-n-roll-aspirant-to-folk-music-legend.

13. Eriksmoen.

14. Eriksmoen.

15. Eriksmoen.

16. Ed Bradley, "Bob Dylan Gives Rare Interview," *60 Minutes*, CBS News, December 5, 2004, https://www.cbsnews.com/news/60-minutes-bob-dylan -rare-interview-2004/.

17. Bob Dylan, *Chronicles*, vol. 1 (New York: Simon & Schuster, 2004), 288.

18. See Sam Kemp, "Why Did Bob Dylan Change His Name? Exploring Anti-Semitism and Acceptance in 1960s Showbusiness," *Far Out Magazine*, January 28, 2022, https://faroutmagazine.co.uk/why-did-bob-dylan-change-his -name-anti-semitism/.

19. See Eriksmoen, "After a Summer in Fargo."

20. Anthony Scaduto, "Bob Dylan: An Intimate Biography, Part One," *Rolling Stone*, March 2, 1972, https://www.rollingstone.com/music/music-news/bob -dylan-an-intimate-biography-part-one-244147/.

21. Scaduto.

22. Patrick Filbin, "Read Bob Dylan's Full MusiCares Person of the Year Speech," American Songwriter, https://americansongwriter.com/read-bob -dylans-full-musicares-person-year-speech/.

23. Billy Heller, "How Bob Dylan Talked His Way into His First Recording Session 60 Years Ago," *New York Post*, November 17, 2021, https://nypost.com /2021/11/17/how-bob-dylan-landed-his-first-recording-session-60-years-ago/.

24. Heller.

25. Heller.

26. Clinton Heylin, *Bob Dylan: The Recording Sessions, 1960–1994* (New York: St. Martin's Press, 1995), 8.

27. Scaduto, "Bob Dylan: An Intimate Biography, Part One."

28. Scaduto.

29. Scaduto.

30. *No Direction Home.*

31. Pearce Marchbank, ed., *Bob Dylan in His Own Words* (New York: Quick Fox, 1978), 53.

32. See Evan Andrews, "The Day Dylan Went Electric," History Channel, August 26, 2018, https://www.history.com/news/the-day-dylan-went-electric.

33. Andrews.

34. Andrews.

35. See Anthony Scaduto, "Bob Dylan: An Intimate Biography, Part Two," *Rolling Stone*, March 16, 1972, https://www.rollingstone.com/music/music-news /bob-dylan-an-intimate-biography-part-two-237760/.

36. Kevin Rutherford, "Bob Dylan Scores First-Ever No. 1 Song on a Billboard Chart with 'Murder Most Foul,'" *Billboard*, April 8, 2020, https://www.billboard .com/pro/bob-dylan-murder-most-foul-first-number-one-song-chart/.

37. Cott, ed., *Bob Dylan: The Essential Interviews*, 153.

38. Cott, 338.

39. Cott, 41.

40. Cott, 107.

41. See "Bob Dylan Records 'Blowin' in the Wind,'" History Channel, July 7, 2020, https://www.history.com/this-day-in-history/bob-dylan-records-blowin-in -the-wind.

42. Cott, ed., *Bob Dylan: The Essential Interviews*, 62.

43. Cott, 54.

44. Cott, 184.

45. Cott, 340.

46. See Bob Spitz, *Dylan: A Biography* (New York: W. W. Norton, 1991), 241.

47. Cott, ed., *Bob Dylan: The Essential Interviews*, 55.

48. Cott, 329.

49. Dylan, *Chronicles*, vol. 1, 238–239. Dylan's "It Ain't Me Babe" was much influenced by Niles.

50. Bob Dylan, interview by Martin Bronstein, February 20, 1966, Montreal, https://alldylan.com/feb-20-1966-bob-dylan-martin-bronstein-interview -montreal-audio/.

51. Cott, ed., *Bob Dylan: The Essential Interviews*, 338.

52. Cott, 339.

53. Harold Bloom, *The Western Canon* (Boston: Houghton Mifflin Harcourt, 1994), 11.

Notes

Chapter 9

1. Mark Brown, "The Letters, Cards and Poems of People Facing the Enormity of War," *Guardian*, June 18, 2014, https://www.theguardian.com /world/2014/jun/18/first-world-war-exhibition-british-library-letters-poetry.

2. Arthur Conan Doyle, *The New Revelation* (New York: George H. Doran Co., 1918), vi.

3. "Arthur Conan Doyle's Interest in Spiritualism," *The Victorian Web*, November 14, 2013, https://victorianweb.org/authors/doyle/spiritualism.html.

4. "Oliver Joseph Lodge," *New World Encyclopedia*, https://www .newworldencyclopedia.org/entry/Oliver_Joseph_Lodge.

5. Oliver Lodge, *Raymond, or, Life and Death* (New York: George H. Doran Co., 1916).

6. "Oliver Joseph Lodge."

7. See Robert Michael Brain, "Materialising the Medium: Ectoplasm and the Quest for Supra-Normal Biology in Fin-de-Siècle Science and Art," in *Vibratory Modernism*, eds. Anthony Enns and Shelley Trower (London: Palgrave Macmillan, 2013), 115.

8. See Kristin Tablang, "Thomas Edison, B. C. Forbes and the Mystery of the Spirit Phone," *Forbes*, October 25, 2019, https://www.forbes.com/sites /kristintablang/2019/10/25/thomas-edison-bc-forbes-mystery-spirit-phone /?sh=7629cf9529ad.

9. David Jaher, *The Witch of Lime Street* (New York: Broadway Books, 2016), 23.

10. Jaher, 31.

11. Jaher, 33.

12. Jaher, 27.

13. Jaher, 65.

14. Jaher, 42.

15. Jaher, 70–71.

16. Jaher, 70–71.

17. Jaher, 82.

18. Jaher, 76.

19. Jaher, 77.

20. Jaher, 75.

21. Jaher, 78.

22. Jaher, 87.

23. Jaher, 103.

24. Jaher, 122.

25. Jaher, 84.

26. Jaher, 15.

27. Jaher, 54.

28. Jaher, 404.

29. Jaher, 84.
30. Jaher, 84.
31. Jaher, 84–85.
32. Jaher, 85.
33. Jaher, 102.
34. Jaher, 100.
35. Jaher, 102.
36. Jaher, 102.
37. Jaher, 124.
38. Jaher, 126.
39. Jaher, 127.
40. Jaher, 171.
41. Jaher, 171.
42. Jaher, 161.
43. Jaher, 196.
44. Jaher, 166.
45. Jaher, 199.
46. Jaher, 208.
47. Jaher, 207.
48. Jaher, 203.
49. Jaher, 213.
50. Massimo Polidoro, *Final Séance* (Amherst, NY: Prometheus Books, 2001), 137.
51. Jaher, *The Witch of Lime Street*, 224.
52. Jaher, 221.
53. Jaher, 225.
54. Crandon to Conan Doyle, June 6, 1924, on file at Harry Ransom Center, University of Texas, Austin.
55. Jaher, *The Witch of Lime Street*, 231.
56. Jaher, 232.
57. Jaher, 234.
58. Jaher, 241.
59. "Margery Pamphlet," *American Experience*, PBS, https://www.pbs.org/wgbh/americanexperience/features/houdini-margery-pamphlet/.
60. Jaher, *The Witch of Lime Street*, 268.
61. "Margery Pamphlet.
62. Jaher, *The Witch of Lime Street*, 268.
63. "Timeline of Houdini's Life," *American Experience*, PBS, https://www.pbs.org/wgbh/americanexperience/features/houdini-timeline/.
64. Mark Wyman Richardson and Charles Stanton Hill, *Margery, Harvard, Veritas: A Study in Psychics* (Boston: Blanchard Printing Co., 1925), 10.
65. Jaher, *The Witch of Lime Street*, 368.
66. Jaher, 330.

Notes

67. Jaher, 378.

68. Jaher, 393.

69. Jaher, 357.

70. Polidoro, *Final Séance*, 234.

71. Jaher, *The Witch of Lime Street*, 404.

72. Jaher, 246.

73. Jaher, 402.

74. Jaher, 341.

75. William Kalush and Larry Sloman, The Secret Life of Houdini (New York: Atria, 2007), 491..

76. Kalush and Sloman, 495.

77. Jaher, *The Witch of Lime Street*, 377.

78. Jaher, 410.

Chapter 10

1. Ayn Rand, *The Fountainhead* (New York: Bobbs-Merrill Co., 1943), 9.

2. Rand, 743.

3. Rand, 113.

4. Ayn Rand, *For the New Intellectual* (New York: Random House, 1961), 77.

5. Rand, *The Fountainhead*, 738.

6. Rand, 738.

7. Ed Kilgore, "Donald Trump's Role Model Is an Ayn Rand Character," *New York Magazine*, April 12, 2016, https://nymag.com/intelligencer/2016/04/trumps-role-model-is-an-ayn-rand-character.html.

8. Lisa Duggan, "How Ayn Rand Became the Spirit of Our Time," *Literary Hub*, May 31, 2019, https://lithub.com/how-ayn-rand-became-the-spirit-of-our-time/.

9. Duggan.

10. *The Fountainhead*, Ayn Rand Institute, https://aynrand.org/novels/the-fountainhead/.

11. *Atlas Shrugged*, Ayn Rand Institute, https://aynrand.org/novels/atlas-shrugged/.

12. Shana Lebowitz, Allana Akhtar, and May Teng, "16 Books Steve Jobs Always Turned to for Inspiration," *Business Insider*, February 24, 2021, https://www.businessinsider.com/steve-jobs-reading-list-favorite-books-2015-10; Anna Wiener, "What Is It about Peter Thiel?" *New Yorker*, October 27, 2021, https://www.newyorker.com/news/letter-from-silicon-valley/what-is-it-about-peter-thiel; Andreas Kluth, "Elon Musk and the Confessions of an Ayn Rand Reader," *Washington Post*, November 27, 2022, https://www.washingtonpost.com/business/elon-musk-and-the-confessions-of-an-ayn-rand-reader/2022/11/27/0587ba4c-6e32-11ed-8619-0b92f0565592_story.html ("Jeff Bezos and quite a few other . . . tech tycoons adulate Ayn Rand").

13. Jonathan Freedland, "The New Age of Ayn Rand: How She Won Over Trump and Silicon Valley," *Guardian*, April 10, 2017, https://www.theguardian

.com/books/2017/apr/10/new-age-ayn-rand-conquered-trump-white-house
-silicon-valley.

14. Jan Frel, "Ryan's Ayn Rand Obsession," *Salon*, August 13, 2012, https://
www.salon.com/2012/08/13/ryans_ayn_rand_obsession_salpart/.

15. Jennifer Burns, *Goddess of the Market* (Oxford: Oxford University Press,
2009), 4.

16. Michael Shermer, "The Real Rogue Warrior: Ayn Rand, Not Sarah Palin,"
Huffpost, May 25, 2011, https://www.huffpost.com/entry/the-real-rogue-warrior
-ay_b_367954.

17. Lisa Duggan, *Mean Girl: Ayn Rand and the Culture of Greed* (Oakland:
University of California Press, 2019), 13.

18. Duggan, *Mean Girl*, 15.

19. Nathaniel Branden, *Judgment Day: My Years with Ayn Rand* (Boston:
Houghton Mifflin, 1989), 46.

20. Duggan, *Mean Girl*, 18.

21. Branden, *Judgment Day*, 62.

22. Duggan, 21–22.

23. Duggan, 20.

24. Duggan, 22.

25. Duggan, 33.

26. Duggan, 34.

27. Jennifer A. Grossman, "5 Things to Know about Frank O'Connor, Ayn
Rand's Husband," *The Atlas Society*, November 9, 2016, https://archive
.atlassociety.org/index.php/commentary/commentary-blog/6101-5-things-to
-know-about-frank-o-connor-ayn-rand-s-husband.

28. Duggan, *Mean Girl*, 110.

29. Duggan, *Mean Girl*, 30–43.

30. See generally Jennifer Burns, "The Three 'Furies' of Libertarianism: Rose
Wilder Lane, Isabel Paterson, and Ayn Rand," *Journal of American History* 102,
no. 3 (December 2015): 746–774.

31. Duggan, *Mean Girl*, 44.

32. Ayn Rand, "The Individualist Manifesto" (unpublished manuscript,
1941).

33. Duggan, *Mean Girl*, 39.

34. Duggan, 51.

35. Duggan, 39.

36. Duggan, 41.

37. Duggan, 54.

38. Duggan, 56.

39. Duggan, 56.

40. Duggan, 56.

41. Duggan, 56.

42. Duggan, 56.

Notes

43. Steve Chawkins, "Nathaniel Branden Dies at 84; Acolyte and Lover of Ayn Rand," *Los Angeles Times*, December 9, 2014, https://www.baltimoresun.com /la-me-nathaniel-branden-20141209-story.html.

44. Branden, *Judgment Day*, 36–37.

45. Anne C. Heller, *Ayn Rand and the World She Made* (New York: Anchor Books, 2010), 222.

46. Barbara Branden, *The Passion of Ayn Rand* (New York: Doubleday, 1986), 234.

47. Duggan, *Mean Girl*, 56.

48. Duggan, 56.

49. Duggan, 56.

50. Branden, *Judgment Day*, 118.

51. Heller, *Ayn Rand and the World She Made*, 243.

52. Branden, *Judgment Day*, 133.

53. Branden, 134.

54. Nathaniel Branden's *Judgment Day: My Years with Ayn Rand* is a riveting account, lurid and full of insights into this relationship. Excellent biographies are Heller, *Ayn Rand and the World She Made*, and Burns, *Goddess of the Market*.

55. Ayn Rand, *Atlas Shrugged* (New York: Random House, 1957).

56. Branden, *Judgment Day*, 176.

57. Whittaker Chambers, "Big Sister Is Watching You," *National Review*, December 28, 1957, https://www.nationalreview.com/2005/01/big-sister -watching-you-whittaker-chambers/.

58. Duggan, *Mean Girl*, 66.

59. Branden, *Judgment Day*, 206.

60. Branden, 81.

61. Duggan, *Mean Girl*, 67.

62. Duggan, 86.

63. Branden, *Judgment Day*, 226.

64. Branden, 359.

65. Branden, 360.

66. Branden, 326.

67. Branden, 341.

68. Branden, 336.

69. Branden, 355.

70. Duggan, *Mean Girl*, 73.

71. Duggan, 79.

72. Duggan, 80.

73. Duggan, 80.

74. Rand, *The Fountainhead*, 149.

75. See Robert Nozick, "On the Randian Argument," *Pacific Philosophical Quarterly* 52, no. 2 (1971): 282–304.

76. Rand, *The Fountainhead*, 17.

77. Rand, 9.

78. Duggan, *Mean Girl*, 5.

79. Branden, *Judgment Day*, 403.

Chapter 11

1. Philip Norman, *Paul McCartney: The Life* (New York: Little, Brown, 2016), 156.

2. Mark Lewisohn, *Tune In: The Beatles, All These Years* (New York: Crown Archetype, 2013).

3. Accounts of the Beatles early days differ in some details, but I do my best here to capture what seems to be the most plausible account of the critical moments.

4. Lewisohn, *Tune In*, 397–489.

5. Lewisohn, 514.

6. Lewisohn, 505.

7. How well they did in their Decca test is disputed; see Norman, *Paul McCartney: The Life*, 147.

8. Lewisohn, *Tune In*, 558.

9. Lewisohn, 558.

10. Lewisohn, 562.

11. Lewisohn, 591.

12. Norman, *Paul McCartney: The Life*, 152.

13. Lewisohn, *Tune In*, 571.

14. Lewisohn, 766.

15. Norman, *Paul McCartney: The Life*, 157.

16. See Philip Norman, *John Lennon: The Life* (New York: Ecco, 2008), 281.

17. Lewisohn, *Tune In*, 717.

18. Norman, *Paul McCartney: The Life*, 283.

19. Norman, 287.

20. Norman, 287.

21. "The Beatles," Official Charts, accessed January 11, 2024, https://www.officialcharts.com/artist/10363/beatles/.

22. Lewisohn, *Tune In*, 717.

23. Norman, *Paul McCartney: The Life*, 289.

24. Norman, 290.

25. Norman, 292.

26. Lewisohn, *Tune In*, 803.

Epilogue

1. Jill Lepore, *Book of Ages* (New York: Knopf, 2013), 218.

2. Alex Bell et al., "Who Becomes an Inventor in America? The Importance of Exposure to Innovation," *Quarterly Journal of Economics* 134, no. 2 (2019): 647–713.

Notes

3. A superb, moving treatment is Robert H. Frank, *Success and Luck: Good Fortune and the Myth of Meritocracy* (Princeton: Princeton University Press, 2016).

4. John Stuart Mill, *The Subjection of Women* (Philadelphia: J. B. Lippincott & Co., 1869), 13, 30–31.

5. H. J. Jackson, *Those Who Write for Immortality* (New Haven: Yale University Press, 2015), xxii.

INDEX

Index

Index

Index

Index

Index

ACKNOWLEDGMENTS

The story of this book is, in a way, a miniature version of what the book is about. In 2021, I worked as a Senior Counselor in the Department of Homeland Security. Transitioning to a more part-time role in 2022, I was free to write again, and I started to look for new projects. I just happened to come across a notice: the University of Liverpool Press was starting a new journal, called *The Journal of Beatles Studies*. I love the Beatles (did you know?), and with trepidation and delight, I thought that I might try to write for that journal. I wrote the editor, Holly Tessler, with an idea, which was to compare the Beatles' masterpiece, "Norwegian Wood," with Bob Dylan's much edgier "Fourth Time Around," which is in a way a knockoff of "Norwegian Wood," in a way a parody, and in a way a dazzling act of one-upmanship. Maybe that would be interesting? Very generously, Holly encouraged me to give it a try.

What I wrote was horrible. It was so amateurish! So I tried something altogether different, on the wellsprings of Beatlemania. Holly didn't seem to hate it, and she sent it to peer reviewers, who had superb comments, and who also seemed not to hate it. I posted an early version of that little paper on the Social Science Research Network—which I love dearly, but which is not exactly the place to post something if you seek a large audience. To my utter astonishment, and I am sure through a series of coincidences, the paper attracted attention. The paper did not become famous, I hasten to add, but it was discussed in the *New York Times, Scientific*

Acknowledgments

American, and the *Guardian*. Soon thereafter, some editors asked me if I might want to turn it into a book. My answer was not no. And here we are.

I am grateful to many people for their help, and I will single out just a few. Thanks go first and foremost to Jeff Kehoe for terrific comments and for valuable help at multiple stages. Jill Lepore offered exceptionally valuable suggestions that reoriented the book in significant ways. Four reviewers offered a host of important ideas for improvement. Duncan Watts, a friend and one of my heroes, was also a reviewer. He has written brilliantly on this topic, and I owe him a great debt; I am also thankful to him for a fun and illuminating conversation at a time when I was a bit stuck. Tyler Cowen, who knows everything, was a terrific discussant (and a reviewer as well). Robert Frank, also a friend and hero, has done superb work that helped orient my discussion.

Lise Clavel, Howard Fishman, Daniel Kahneman, Géraldine Schwarz, Geoffrey Stone, and Richard Thaler have been generous enough to discuss some of the underlying issues with me. Special thanks to Fishman for his amazing book on Connie Converse, which was a great help here, and special thanks also to Schwarz for discussions and references on memory. Nick Caputo, Ethan Judd, Sarah Toth, and Victoria Yu provided superb research assistance. Special thanks to Yu for incredible work in bringing this book to completion.

Holly Tessler, mentioned above, is a sine qua non, and she was kind enough to host me for a terrific visit at the University of Liverpool; the discussion there was exceedingly valuable. Sarah Chalfant, my agent, was a wise counselor throughout. Samantha Power, my wife, was supportive of, amused by, and maybe even enthusiastic about this project, or at least about my enthusiasm for it. She had plenty of thoughts, which made their way into these pages (and she also allowed me to talk about her, a tiny bit, in chapter 1). Thanks too to Harvard Law School, its Program on Behavioral Economics, and its amazing dean, John Manning, for help and support of multiple kinds.

I have drawn on (while substantially revising, and sometimes making fundamental changes in) the following material, and I am most grateful for permission to do so:

- for chapters 1 and 11 (and occasionally elsewhere):

  - "Beatlemania: On Informational Cascades and Spectacular Success," Journal of Beatles Studies 97 (2022)

- for chapter 6:

  - The World According to Star Wars, 2nd edition (New York: Dey Street Books, 2018). Particular thanks to Dey Street Books and Simon & Schuster for permission to draw on material from that book here

- for chapter 8:

  - "Marvelous Belief," Los Angeles Review of Books (September 21, 2020)

- for chapter 9:

  - "She Was Houdini's Greatest Challenge," New York Review of Books (December 17, 2015)

- for chapter 10:

  - "The Siren of Selfishness," New York Review of Books (April 9, 2020)

ABOUT THE AUTHOR

CASS R. SUNSTEIN is currently the Robert Walmsley University Professor at Harvard. He is the founder and director of the Program on Behavioral Economics and Public Policy at Harvard Law School. In 2018, he received the Holberg Prize from the government of Norway, sometimes described as the equivalent of the Nobel Prize for law and the humanities. In 2020, the World Health Organization appointed him as Chair of its technical advisory group on Behavioural Insights and Sciences for Health. From 2009 to 2012, he was Administrator of the White House Office of Information and Regulatory Affairs, and after that, he served on the President's Review Board on Intelligence and Communications Technologies and on the Pentagon's Defense Innovation Board. Mr. Sunstein has testified before congressional committees on many subjects, and he has advised officials at the United Nations, the European Commission, the World Bank, and many nations on issues of law and public policy. He has served as an adviser to the Behavioural Insights Team in the United Kingdom.

Mr. Sunstein is the author of hundreds of articles and dozens of books, including the bestseller *Nudge: Improving Decisions about Health, Wealth, and Happiness* (with Richard H. Thaler, 2008).